HELP!

For Teachers of Young Children

D1456686

To Al

who is always there to help me

HELP!

For Teachers of Young Children

Gwen Snyder Kaltman

88 Tips
to Develop Children's
SOCIAL SKILLS
and Create Positive
**TEACHER-FAMILY
RELATIONSHIPS**

CORWIN PRESS
A SAGE Publications Company
Thousand Oaks, California

For information:

Corwin Press
A Sage Publications Company
2455 Teller Road
Thousand Oaks, California 91320
www.corwinpress.com

Sage Publications Ltd
1 Oliver's Yard
55 City Road
London EC1Y 1SP
United Kingdom

Sage Publications India Pvt. Ltd.
B-42, Panchsheel Enclave
Post Box 4109
New Delhi 110 017 India

Printed in the United States of America on acid-free paper

Library of Congress Cataloging-in-Publication Data

Kaltman, Gwen Snyder.
Help! for teachers of young children : 88 tips to develop children's social skills and create positive teacher-family relationships / Gwen Snyder Kaltman.
    p. cm.
Includes bibliographical references and index.
ISBN 1-4129-2442-1 (cloth) — ISBN 1-4129-2443-X (pbk.)
   1. Education, Preschool. 2. Social skills. 3. Parent-teacher relationships.
4. Preschool teachers—Training of. I. Title.
LB1140.2 .K314 2006
372.21—dc22

                                                    2005010618

05   06   07   08   10   9   8   7   6   5   4   3   2   1

Acquisitions editor:	Stacy Wagner
Copy editor:	Kristin Bergstad
Typesetter:	C&M Digitals (P) Ltd.
Cover Designer:	Rose Storey
Graphic Designer:	Scott Van Atta

Contents

Preface

The Australian Aborigines have the longest continuous living culture on the planet. They have no written language. For over 50,000 years, knowledge has been passed from generation to generation by elders who tell stories as a way of entertaining and, more important, educating their people on proper behavior and customs. Wally of the Anangu people told me that an elder will often create a story using mischievous spirits called Mimis to tactfully get across a message. Following in the tradition of the Aborigines and anyone else who has ever told the story of The Three Little Pigs, I too use stories to both entertain and enlighten. My stories are told to help teachers and parents better understand young children, how to interact with them, and how to teach them.

I hope you find the stories so interesting and entertaining that you keep turning the pages because you just can't wait to see the next story. I'd like to suggest that when you are done reading the book you do not put it away on a shelf. Instead, choose a topic that you are comfortable with and reread that chapter. As you do, take the time to think and reflect. How does the material apply to you in your circumstances? What could you try, what could you improve on, how could you modify some of the ideas to fit your particular situation?

Use this book as your own personal mentor. To help you do this, I have included a resource: Creating Your Own Plan for Improvement. Every year your skills and understanding will increase, and your experiences will influence you to see things in a different light. I hope you will use the chapters in this book as mini workshops and refer to them over and over again during the course of your career. My expectations are high; please don't let them frustrate you. Instead, let them inspire you to soar to greater heights.

While what I have written comes from many years of experience in the preschool classroom, my advice is based on established theories and research on child development and learning by psychologists and educators such as Bruner, Dewey, Elkind,

Froebel, Piaget, and Vygotsky. The material in this book is equally applicable for both parents and teachers. We are, after all, on the same team.

I cannot answer all of the questions you may have or predict the problems you will face in the future. I can only offer some of the principles that have guided me over the years. Try to empower young children and give them the time and freedom to explore a rich, safe environment. Recognize that play for the child is not a diversion, but an important way to learn about the world. Understand and respect the children's interests and developmental level. If we are sensitive and observant, they will show us the way.

This book focuses on developing children's social skills and creating positive teacher-family relationships. I have also written a companion volume, *More Help! For Teachers of Young Children*, that addresses the equally important subjects of promoting intellectual development and creativity.

Nuts and Bolts

Each chapter in this book contains a brief introduction followed by a number of stories. After each story, I provide help and questions for you to ask yourself. At the end of each chapter is a section called "Try This" that contains a few suggestions for you to try. I hope these will inspire you to think of many more things you can do with children.

Child care provider, care giver, early childhood specialist, preschool teacher, and *educarer* are just some of the terms frequently used to describe people who work with young children. To keep things simple I use the term *teacher* throughout this book. I use the terms *center* and *school* interchangeably rather than differentiating between them. Finally, to avoid the grammatical awkwardness of "he or she" I use one gender or the other when referring to children. I chose to use the pronoun *she* when referring to a teacher or director because the majority of them are females. My apologies for this slight to the dedicated and much valued men who also work with young children.

In all instances the names have been changed to protect the innocent, the guilty, and me from a lot of phone calls.

My mother taught me a simple philosophy of life. I can still hear her saying, "Don't just take, you should also give back; lend a helping hand to the next guy." I hope you think this book is a helping hand.

Acknowledgments

Choose a job you love and you will never have to work a day in your life.

—Confucius

I had not planned to spend my life working with young children, but the faculty of the University of Maryland introduced me to the wonderful world of early childhood education and from then on I was hooked. I consider myself incredibly lucky to have been taught by such outstanding leaders in the field as James L. Hymes, Jr., Sarah Lou Leeper, Lillian Willse Brown, and Joan Moyer.

Jackie Hill welcomed this girl from Brooklyn to Tennessee and gave me the opportunity to teach at Chattanooga State. I also want to express my appreciation to all of the directors, teachers, students, and families I have worked with through the years.

I owe a great deal to my friends and colleagues, Nora Callahan, Arlene Friedland, Cindy Goodman, Paula Ott, Jo Robbins, and especially Judy Zimmerman, who took the time to read an early draft of the manuscript. They gave me the benefit of their experience and wise council.

I am indebted to Faye Zucker, the executive editor of Corwin Press, for her support. The staff at Corwin Press has worked hard to bring this project to fruition. Their efforts, especially those of Kristin Bergstad, are gratefully acknowledged. Stacy Wagner has been a staunch advocate from the start. Her suggestions and help with the manuscript are deeply appreciated. I could not have wished for a better editor.

Last but not least I want to thank my husband Al and my sons Blaine and Mylan. Their advice and encouragement were truly invaluable.

Corwin Press acknowledges the important contributions of the following reviewers:

Gloria Hearn
Educational Consultant
Hearn & Hearn Consultants
Pineville, LA

S. Jackie Hill
Associate Professor & Early
  Childhood Education
  Program Coordinator
Chattanooga State Technical
Community College, TN

Ruth R. Kennedy
Assistant Professor
Bloomsburg University of
Pennsylvania

Kathleen McGinn
Director of Child Development
  Programs
Colton Joint Unified School
District, CA

Joan Moyer
Professor Emeritus
Arizona State University

Marilyn Segal
Director of Academics, Mailman
Segal Institute for Early
  Childhood Studies
Nova Southeastern University, FL

Joan Franklin Smutny
Director of The Center for Gifted
National-Louis University,
Chicago IL

Catheryn Weitman
Professor
Barry University, FL

Judy Zimmerman
Executive Director, Mailman Segal
Institute for Early Childhood
  Studies
Nova Southeastern University, FL

About the Author

 **Gwen Snyder Kaltman** has spent more than 25 years working with young children, their parents and teachers. She is the author of *More Help! For Teachers of Young Children: 99 Tips to Promote Intellectual Development and Creativity.* She earned her BS and MEd in Early Childhood Education from the University of Maryland, and has been a preschool teacher, director, college instructor, and educational trainer in various parts of the country. She has also been a validator for the National Academy of Early Childhood Programs, the accreditation division of the National Association for the Education of Young Children.

Kaltman has worked with young children in Connecticut, Delaware, Georgia, Maryland, Massachusetts, New York, Tennessee, and Virginia. She has trained teachers working in Head Start programs in Chattanooga, Tennessee, and rural Georgia and in child care centers and preschools in the suburbs of New York City and Washington, D.C. She has observed preschool classes in such diverse places as China, Easter Island, Greenland, India, Malta, Mongolia, Tibet, Tanzania, Venezuela, and native villages above the Arctic Circle and along the Amazon and Sepik rivers.

Born and raised in the Bedford Stuyvesant section of Brooklyn, New York, she has been married for over 30 years. While it is true that her gray hairs started growing when she was in high school, she attributes most of them to her two sons.

PART I

DEVELOPING CHILDREN'S SOCIAL SKILLS

1

"Yada, Yada, Yada"

Communicating Effectively With the Young Child

The illusion that communication has successfully taken place, when in fact it hasn't, can be a major problem in business, personal relationships, and of course adult/child relationships. Communicating with young children involves much more than words. Long before vocabulary enters the picture, children are fluent in voice tone and body language. A sincere smile or soothing tone communicates volumes to them.

1. Use nonverbal communication

A PAT ON THE ARM

On a flight to Orlando, a young boy traveling alone was in the seat next to me. He was about eight years old, the age when a baseball cap appears to be glued permanently to the head. After the usual "Where are you going, how long will you be there?" questions, I decided to settle in and read my magazine. For a few minutes he played with his handheld electronic game. After he had asked me for the third time, "What time is it? When will we be there?" I offered to play a game with him. Forever the schoolteacher, I suggested the spelling game Hangman. It turned out to be challenging for me, as his creative way of spelling words such as *green* with three E's (greene) really stumped me. After about 15 minutes of good fun and sharing, this little fellow very carefully reached out to touch my arm. His touch said many things to me. This was not a gesture of curiosity, but rather an attempt to show his friendship.

HELP!

 Touch and nonverbal gestures are important ways to communicate at any age. We can communicate approval and positive feelings without using words. For infants, holding, patting, and gentle rubbing of the back or arms should be a part of the daily routine. With older children try:

- ☆ Wink of an eye
- ☆ High-five handshake
- ☆ Squeeze of a shoulder
- ☆ A pat on the head
- ☆ Nod of the head
- ☆ Thumbs up
- ☆ And best of all, a broad smile

ASK YOURSELF:

 Do you use nonverbal communication?

Do you communicate positive feelings to children by your physical presence and body language?

2. Talk frequently
to infants and toddlers

SILENCE IS NOT GOLDEN

The heat index was 101. I was sitting on a bench waiting for a bus. After a few minutes, a mother pushing a stroller with an adorable infant sat down next to me. She smiled and said hello. For the next 20 minutes this mother tickled her child's toes, clapped his hands together, and snuggled her head into his tummy, all of which delighted the child. This loving physical interaction was done in silence. The mother never spoke a word. When the bus arrived I had to bite my tongue not to say to her, "You love your child so much, why don't you talk to him?"

HELP!

We should talk frequently to young children. Hearing the spoken word is vital to a child's development.

I find it odd that some people will readily talk to pet cats or dogs, but seem to feel awkward talking to a very young child. I realize having a conversation with an infant or toddler can be like talking to a wall, but we have to find ways to expose them to the spoken word. As a minimum, I would recommend chatting about the activities you are doing. Like a radio announcer reports a baseball game: "Now the batter steps up to the plate, swings the bat a few times and digs his heels into the dirt." We can talk about what we are doing. "I am going to tickle Evan's little toes. Let's clap your lovely little hands together. Look out; I'm going to snuggle against your tummy." When you think about it, many everyday mundane activities can provide opportunities to talk to very young children. For example, "I am getting the clean diaper out of the box, I will remove the old smelly diaper, wash your bottom, and put on a fresh clean one with pretty blue stars, and this will make you more comfortable."

It does not matter if you talk to an infant or toddler about your philosophy of life, the dreams you have, the cold weather, or the plot of the last movie you saw. The content of your speech, as long as the tone is not scaring the child, is not significant. If you do not have much to say, you could consider reading a magazine or book out loud, any book. Talk about whatever is easiest for you, but by all means TALK.

Copying and thereby reinforcing the sounds an infant makes is another important activity.

ASK YOURSELF:

Do you remember to talk and interact with infants and toddlers throughout the day, not just at feeding or diaper-changing times?

Are you responsive to the sounds an infant makes?

3. Get down to the child's eye level

EYEBALL TO EYEBALL

One of my more memorable blind dates was with a very, very tall fellow. The first part of the evening was awkward. Even when I tried standing on tippy-toe, communication was severely limited. I remember feeling as though I were trying to talk with an armpit. It wasn't until we sat down at a table for some pizza that I finally felt I could see his face and have a reasonable conversation.

HELP!

Young children read faces. When communicating, try to drop down to their eye level. In this way you can be sure you are talking with them, rather than at them. Eye to eye is much better than toe to toe.

My date was on his way to try out for a major league baseball team. He made it, and played for the Baltimore Orioles. He was six feet four inches tall and weighed 230 lbs. I am five feet tall, and my weight is strictly confidential!

ASK YOURSELF:

Do you position yourself to be at the children's eye level when you talk to them?

4. Use positive language

YES MEANS EVERYTHING

The two-year-old class is out on the playground, and all the swings are occupied. When Juanita asks to go on a swing, the teacher replies, "No, all the swings are busy now. We have to wait for someone to get off." It is a logical response to the request, but before the sentence is half spoken Juanita throws herself to the ground shrieking and protesting. The teacher smiles and responds, "It is hard for two-year-olds to learn to share."

HELP!

 With two-year-olds, whose basic vocabulary consists of NO, NO, and MINE, communication needs to be handled very diplomatically. The child heard the word "no" (request denied) and never bothered to hear the rest of the teacher's sentence. A response that begins with the word "yes" is likely to fare much better: "Yes, you can have the very next turn, as soon as Howard is done," or "Yes, we take turns and you will be on soon. Why don't you play in the sandbox, and I will call you when it is your turn." We are saying the same thing, but in a positive rather than a negative way. This also works when communicating with adults.

ASK YOURSELF:

Do you talk to children in a positive way?

Do you minimize your use of the word "no"?

5. Be more responsive to what a child does than to what he says

NO MEANS NOTHING

James, a two-year-old, was wandering around the classroom when the teacher said, "James, will you please go wash your hands now? We are getting ready for snack time." James turned to face the teacher, put his hands on his hips, stuck his chin out defiantly, and in a very loud voice said, "No." He then promptly turned around and went to the sink to wash his hands.

HELP!

 Two-year-olds love to say no. It is such a powerful word that they sometimes use it even when they don't mean it. If you do not respond too quickly, the child will probably do whatever it is you are requesting, after he has had the satisfaction of saying NO. In this type of situation, what the child does is much more important than what he says.

> Do not ask a young child a yes/no question unless you are prepared to live with his answer. To avoid this problem try to present choices, such as, "Do you want to wash right now, or after you put away your toys?" This allows the child to feel powerful, make a decision you are comfortable with, and do it in a positive rather than negative manner.

I really didn't say everything I said.

—Yogi Berra

ASK YOURSELF:

Do you give children opportunities to make decisions you can live with thereby avoiding power struggles, or are they just told what to do?

Are you careful not to respond too quickly when a child says "no"?

6. Offer limited choices

THIRTY-ONE FLAVORS

On a humid August afternoon a mother and her two children were just in front of me in a long line at an ice cream parlor that offered 31 flavors. The mother and the seven-year-old gave their orders quickly, but for the four-year-old it was another story. For the third time the mother began reading off the choices. The child listened attentively and said "Chocolate," after 10 seconds she said "No, I want cherry," five seconds later she tearfully pleaded for rocky road and then again for chocolate. The mother became upset and snarled, "Just make up your mind; tell me, what do you want?" What started out as a happy outing had become a tense situation. Of course, the logical answer to this dilemma is that one should always choose rocky road.

HELP!

Children need to learn how to make decisions, but too many choices to select from can be overwhelming to a young child. Four-year-olds are notorious for indecision. They try to explore all their options, and in so doing often frustrate themselves and the adults around them. We can help by limiting their choices to a manageable level of two or three items. "Do you want to eat pizza or fish sticks?" is easier for a child to respond to than the open ended "What do you want to eat tonight?" Offering limited, rather than unlimited, choices will make life easier for you and the children.

ASK YOURSELF:

Do you offer children limited choices?

Do you respect their choices?

Do you pose questions correctly for the age of the child?

7. Be a language role model

BABY TALK

Mrs. Babble was the new teacher in the toddler room. She was a very caring and affectionate person. The following is just a sample of some of the phrases I heard her use when talking to the children.

Does honsey-wonsey want some yum-yum for his tum-tum?

Does angelsy-wangelsy need to make nap-nap now?

Let's make nicey-nicey with our friendsy-wensies.

HELP!

Being affectionate and using pet names for young children is very different from talking baby talk. Young children will copy speech patterns and emulate what adults say and how they say it. It is important for us to model correct speech.

When children mispronounce a word or say something that is not grammatically correct, rather than correcting them, repeat back what they said in the correct way. For example, when the child says "I et pasketti" you can reply "How nice, you ate spaghetti." By using this subtle approach we are not stifling the children's expression by overtly correcting them. We are helping them by being a good role model.

ASK YOURSELF:

Do you avoid using baby talk?

Do you model correct speech?

8. Use language to influence a child's response to negative events

DON'T GIVE THEM IDEAS

I was sitting in a sandwich shop when two mothers and three young girls came in. The girls appeared to be about three or four years old. Two of the girls were tightly holding strings that had red balloons attached to them. This made removing their jackets a complicated task. As the mother of the child who did not have a balloon started to help her take off her jacket the child asked, "Where is my balloon?" The mother answered, "You don't have it anymore." The child calmly replied, "I want it, where is it?" The mother, starting to get impatient said, "Remember, you let go of the string and lost it. Now don't start crying, but you lost your balloon." The child who up until that time was calm, thought this reply over for a few seconds, and then, of course, began to cry and scream.

HELP!

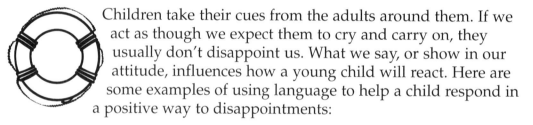 Children take their cues from the adults around them. If we act as though we expect them to cry and carry on, they usually don't disappoint us. What we say, or show in our attitude, influences how a young child will react. Here are some examples of using language to help a child respond in a positive way to disappointments:

☆ When a child falls down we should respond calmly. Try saying something like, "That was a big fall, but you look fine to me." Handled in this manner, the child will take her cue from the adult, and probably pick herself up and continue playing.

☆ A lost toy could be handled by saying, "I know you like that toy. Would you like me to help you look for it?"

☆ If a crayon breaks, you can say, "Your crayon broke, that's okay, it still works, and now you have two."

The adult sets the tone. If we respond to problems as something that can be dealt with, while controlling our emotions, then we are being positive role models for the children. We are teaching by word and example how to deal with the inevitable problems and disappointments that occur in life.

ASK YOURSELF:

Do you stay calm when a child is upset?

Do you use language that encourages children to keep their emotions in check?

Do you encourage children to respond positively when faced with negative situations?

9. Use specific language

WERE YOU A GOOD BOY TODAY?

It can be amusing to watch parents as they drop their children off at school in the morning. Along with hugs and kisses come reminders to "play nice" or "be good." At the end of the day, the children get more hugs and kisses and the inevitable follow-up question: "Were you a good boy today?" It is interesting to watch the children ponder the answer to this. After all, being good can cover a lot of territory. Depending on the parent and child, it may include (but is not limited to)

- ✮ Sharing toys
- ✮ Cooperating at cleanup time
- ✮ Eating your vegetables at lunch
- ✮ Paying attention during story time
- ✮ Not wetting your pants
- ✮ Not crashing the tricycle
- ✮ Not biting or hitting
- ✮ Not crying
- ✮ Not soiling your clothing with paint
- ✮ And watching out for your younger sister

HELP!

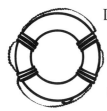 During workshops, when I ask adults, "What does nice mean?" or "What is good?" they have a hard time giving a specific answer. Yet we expect children to understand what we mean when we use all-encompassing phrases such as "be good" or "play nice."

Rather than say to a child that he is a good boy, you should say that it is good or you like it when he helps clean up, waits patiently, or eats his vegetables. We need to highlight the specific behavior that pleases us so the child understands why he is being complimented. Similarly, "take turns," or "be gentle" is much easier for a child to understand than the all-inclusive and vague "play nice" or "be nice."

> If a child is doing something wrong, you should not say that he is bad. Instead tell him that what he is doing is wrong. While we can reject specific behavior, we must always accept the child.

My idea of nice is when I have had a hard day and my husband offers to bring home a pizza for supper. When he offers to take me out to a restaurant, that's good!

ASK YOURSELF:

Do you avoid using generalizations?

When expressing approval or disapproval to a child, do you mention a specific behavior so the child clearly understands, instead of using the all-inclusive phrase "be good"?

Do you say to children who are being noisy and not paying attention at group time, "Excuse me" when you really should say, "Please be quiet I am talking now" or "Please wait for your turn"?

10. Avoid using sarcasm

THE PIANO

As part of our fire safety week the children were learning about fire drills and evacuating the building. Our classroom had two doors, each located at opposite ends of the room. One door led to a long hallway, and the other went directly out onto the playground (a wonderful arrangement). I was concerned that the children would not know which door to go to when the fire alarm rang, so rather than talk about different doors, I told them we would meet by the piano, which was conveniently located right by the door leading out to the playground. I repeated this important message on several occasions. I was confident that the children clearly understood that when there was a fire drill they should go to the piano, and the teachers would be there to help them get outside safely.

One afternoon Laura came over to me with a serious face. She was clearly very concerned and troubled. She said, "What will I do if there is a fire in my house, because we don't have a piano. Where should I go?"

HELP!

Young children tend to interpret language literally, and this can cause them to misunderstand what has been said or to make incorrect generalizations. Like someone who is just starting to learn a new language, they do not understand nuances or sarcasm. Expressions such as "feeling blue," "raining cats and dogs," "having a whale of a time," or "being a bit under the weather" can be confusing to the young child. We must be very careful when we talk to young children to be clear and specific. Our instructions and particularly our humor can be easily misinterpreted. "Dig what I mean?"

If the English language made any sense, lackadaisical would have something to do with a shortage of flowers.

—Doug Larson

ASK YOURSELF:

Do you avoid using sarcasm, adult humor, or language that young children can easily misinterpret?

Do you speak to children in language that is clear and easily understood by them?

11. Engage children in conversation

LET'S CHAT

Josh was a shy child who basically relied on gestures and body language to communicate. He was an expert at pointing his finger and shaking or nodding his head. I was quite startled one day by the sound of his voice interrupting the story I was reading. It was a book about animals getting ready for winter. When I turned the page to show a mouse, he suddenly had many things to say. Obviously an incident in his home involving a mouse had occurred recently. It was such a delight to finally hear him chatter about something.

HELP!

 We should make an extra effort to engage quiet children in conversation to help them learn to communicate and build their self-confidence. When trying to initiate conversation ask open-ended questions that cannot be answered with a simple yes, no, or nod of the head. What children know best and can, therefore, talk about is their immediate environment. They talk about their reality. This includes such topics as:

- ✯ Food
- ✯ Toys
- ✯ Their house
- ✯ Friends
- ✯ Family
- ✯ Pets

I try not to ask about TV shows or movies. I have found that all I get is a rehash of the plot, and as a result, very little real communication with the child occurs.

I do not suggest asking children about mice.

ASK YOURSELF:

Do you make an effort to engage all the children in conversation?

Do you listen attentively when a child speaks, and are you responsive to the child, or do you talk to children only when giving directions?

12. Use props to stimulate conversation

OUT OF THE BLUE

It was a hot day in July. During circle time, the teacher tried to stimulate some interest in the art project, which was going to be a present for the parents. She asked the children, "How do you show caring?" There were a lot of blank looks and fidgeting. After a while someone said, "I go to the beach." The teacher trying to be positive responded, "That's nice." The other children then seemed to understand and chimed in with "I go to the pool" or "I use the sprinkler." Obviously this was not going in the direction the teacher wanted.

HELP!

 I believe it is necessary to plant seeds to help guide children to the topic we want them to think and chat about. Using a picture of a child hugging a parent or a pet, or sharing a toy with someone would have been more effective than just posing a question out of the blue. If you don't have a picture, tell a story: "When I was little, my brother would share his toys with me, and that was very caring." This now gives the children a frame of reference and some idea of what you want to focus on.

ASK YOURSELF:

Do you use pictures, puppets, props, or stories to help children focus on a topic and stimulate conversation?

13. Ask developmentally appropriate questions

WHAT MONTH IS IT?

Mrs. Unoriginal is starting group time with her favorite question.

Teacher: Hey kids, what month is it?

Roberta: It's October.

Teacher: No, that's not it.

Poor Roberta, just when she has figured out the right answer they change the month; it is now early November.

Sophia   (deciding to take a chance, calls out): It's Tuesday.

Simon   (not wanting to be left out of the action chimes in): It is cloudy.

Mrs. Unoriginal senses that this is not going well and tells the children it is the month of November. She then starts the process all over again.

Teacher: What day is today?

Frank: It is Thanksgiving.

Teacher: No, not today.

Simon   (at least being consistent, again says): It is cloudy.

Sooner or later he may guess the right answer; just ask enough questions.

Ira: It's my birthday.

It isn't, but wishful thinking is popular with young children.

HELP!

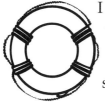

I bet the second most frequently asked question in preschool classrooms is "What month [or day] is it?" I don't understand why this seems to be so very important to teachers. The what-day-or-month question almost always stimulates wild guessing. The teacher rejects answers (and indirectly the children offering them) until some lucky soul guesses correctly, or the teacher gives up and tells everyone the right answer. It would be much more developmentally appropriate to tell the children, "Today is Thursday, and the month is November." The children should be capable of reporting on the weather (go look out the window), and depending on their age and the calendar set-up, perhaps figure out the correct date.

> When asking children questions, we should guard against creating a frenzy of wild guesses. Adults should think carefully about the questions they ask children and try to ensure that they are reasonably capable of responding correctly.

My unscientific poll reveals that the all-time most frequently asked question by a teacher is: "Do you have to go to the bathroom?"

ASK YOURSELF:

Do you ask developmentally appropriate questions of the children in order to encourage thinking?

Do you ask questions that children are capable of responding to correctly, or do your questions stimulate a wild guessing frenzy?

14. Help children tell the truth

INNOCENT LIES

Have you ever noticed that when a teacher wants to stimulate interest in a topic (for instance, a unit on pets), she typically asks "Who has a pet?" Several children will honestly respond with names and information about their pets. Pretty soon everyone is talking about their pets whether they have one or not. All the children want to join in the conversation. After all, not owning a pet puts you at a distinct disadvantage. Similarly, conversations about vacation trips, the strongest brother, or biggest house can fall into a zone of exaggeration.

HELP!

Rather than thinking about this as lying, consider it wishful thinking. Instead of being righteously confrontational, try to react to the child by saying, "If you could have a pet, that is what it would be like." By responding in this fashion, we let the child know that we do not accept the falsehood, but do understand their desire to exaggerate, fantasize, or simply join in the conversation.

♦ Don't overreact when a child tells a lie.

♦ Help children express their ideas in a positive way.

ASK YOURSELF:

Do you help children express themselves in a positive way?

Are you careful not to over-react to a child's white lie?

15. Be honest
and trustworthy

FOR REAL

Tawana and Justin were busy in the dramatic play area. Tawana was the doctor and Justin a somewhat reluctant patient. After a cursory examination of looking with a flashlight in Justin's ear, the doctor announced, "You're sick. You need a shot." As Doctor Tawana busily prepared a syringe, she said in a very reassuring manner, "Now this won't hurt a bit." Justin looking rather nervously at the syringe (which did not have a needle, but did look very scary) replied, "Do you mean this won't hurt a bit like the doctor says, or this won't hurt a bit for real?"

HELP!

Young children are very trusting. It is almost too easy to fool them, and unfortunately many adults take advantage of this trait. The classic example of this is the hurried pediatrician who is often tempted to say, "This won't hurt" when trying to administer an injection. The first time this lie is told, it may keep a child from screaming and wiggling, but most parents will tell you it rarely works more than once. Children learn whom they can and cannot believe. The short-term goal of avoiding a scene is expensive when one thinks about the trust factor that is now damaged. I would much prefer an approach that tells a child, "It is very important to get the medicine, and while it might hurt a little, Mommy will be there. If you hold very still the doctor can be quick, and we will leave right after that."

Remember that when we rely on falsehoods or tricks with children, they are learning from us. Secure bonds of trust and believing far outweigh any short-term advantage one might gain by telling a falsehood to a child in the mistaken hope of avoiding a scene or negative reaction.

When you tell the truth, you don't have to remember what you said.

—Mark Twain

ASK YOURSELF:

Do you avoid using falsehoods or tricks when dealing with children?

16. Understand what the child is asking before answering the question

WHAT WAS THE QUESTION?

My mother used to tell this story: Seven-year-old Tommy comes into the kitchen and says, "Mom, where did I come from?" His mother becomes a little flustered and asks Tommy to wait a minute. She then races into the living room and tells the father, "Tommy is asking where did I come from. It is time to tell him the facts of life." The father dutifully sits down with Tommy and discusses the birds and the bees, complete with little sketches of male and female bodies. Tommy listens intently and when his father is done talking says, "Oh, okay, but what I really want to know is, Billy says he is from New Jersey, where am I from?"

HELP!

Before answering a question try to understand exactly what information the child is looking for. Frequently, young children are satisfied with short answers. Be careful not to over-respond with a long harangue. Explanations to children should be in simple terms that they can understand. We needn't go into lengthy explanations that they may not be interested in yet.

ASK YOURSELF:

Do you take the time to understand what the child wants to know before answering his question?

Do you talk too much?

Do you forget how short a child's attention span is?

Try This

Sit and chat with children at snack and mealtimes.

Call children at home on the telephone. Clear this with their parents first.

Bring in a tape recorder. Record the children talking. After a short time, play the tape back and have the children try to identify who is talking.

Make a stage for puppets out of a box, or just have children stand behind a table and present puppet shows.

Create a TV set out of a box, and make a microphone by putting a tennis ball on a stick. Let the children pretend to be on TV.

Create a story chair or corner where children are the storytellers instead of the adults.

Use a pillowcase to create a surprise bag. Put in an object and ask the children to feel the object through the bag and DESCRIBE it, not identify it. For example, you can put in a ball, stuffed animal, hammer, alarm clock, or fry pan. You are trying to increase vocabulary and have children use words such as *hard, soft, big, small, smooth,* and *round.*

Stimulate conversation and imagination by asking children thought-provoking questions, such as:

☆ If you could do one special magic trick, what would you do?
☆ If you could be an animal, what would you be and what would you do?
☆ If you could be someone else, who would you like to be? Why?

2

"Why Can't You Behave?"

Understanding the Difference Between Discipline and Punishment

Discipline and punishment are very different. Punishment is a negative action; it does not teach children how to behave. Discipline, when used correctly, is a positive process that helps children learn self-control.

I truly believe that the most powerful and effective tool for discipline is LOVE. If a casual acquaintance or stranger says something critical, thoughtless, or rude, an adult generally can shrug it off with an attitude of "What's her problem?" If the criticism comes from a close friend, relative, or parent, we take it much more seriously. We are hurt when someone we care about rejects us or our behavior. In the same way, when children have bonded with adults, they care about the adults' feelings toward them, and how they are being perceived. Children who care about you and what you think of them and their actions will try to please you and respond to your requests. Love and caring are much more potent than stickers and treats.

When you do have to discipline a child always remember to reject the specific behavior, never the child. I completely reject the use of physical violence or shaming children. The negative lessons that they learn from such attempts at discipline are harmful.

You will not be effective if you are constantly criticizing a child. You must decide what is really important. Choose what you want to emphasize, and learn to look the other way at minor offenses that can be addressed later. Otherwise, you may overwhelm the child and run the risk of her deciding it is just too hard to please you.

Our expectations of children's behavior should be based on their developmental level. If an adult uses the word NO with great frequency, it is an indication that the environment is inappropriate or the expectations for the children are beyond their current stage of development.

Providing a good environment with developmentally appropriate expectations of children will go a long way toward helping to minimize behavior problems. However, most teachers understand that there is no magic pill or simple answer to discipline problems. The only thing you can control is your actions. Every child is unique, and every adult is unique. We come with our own experiences and perceptions, which color our responses to situations. I offer you some of my experiences, and how they affect the way I deal with young children in the most difficult of circumstances.

> *You can learn many things from your children.*
> *How much patience you have, for instance.*
>
> —Franklin Jones

17. Control your emotions

DON'T BANG THE FRY PAN

My younger son taught English to eight-year-olds in China. He tells a story about doing a vocabulary lesson on items found in the kitchen. He brought to class a plate, fork, glass, spoon, and fry pan. It was the last week of school, the temperature in the classroom was above 90 degrees, and the children were not paying attention. They were busy chatting or generally misbehaving. He lost his cool and in frustration picked up the fry pan and banged it several times on the desk. Now that he had their attention, he asked them why they were chatting so much and that became the topic for the lesson that day.

HELP!

We are all human. There will be moments when some incident pushes you beyond the level of self-control an adult should have. Pace yourself; try to learn to recognize when you are reaching the overload point. An angry, out-of-control adult should never deal with children. Give yourself a moment to calm down. If no one is in physical danger, try to remove yourself from the situation. Stepping into another room or getting a breath of fresh air can help you maintain your self-control. A short delay can mean the difference between a calm, rational response that provides the child with a positive learning experience or an angry one that has a negative impact.

The best remedy for anger is delay.

—Seneca

ASK YOURSELF:

Do you control your temper?

Are you careful not to intimidate or frighten the children?

18. Have a consistent approach

WE NEED A GAME PLAN

Four-year-old Sara Jane was a born negotiator. I'm sure by now she is happily working in the diplomatic corps. She was the type of child who rarely accepted "no" for an answer. If she did not get the response she wanted from an adult, she would merely rephrase the question or go to another adult to try to get a different answer.

One day Sara Jane asked me if she could have the play dough. I explained that there wasn't enough time since we were going to be cleaning up shortly, but I would definitely put it out tomorrow. Not happy with that answer she went over to the assistant teacher and again asked about using play dough. The assistant teacher, realizing it was almost cleanup time, also denied the request. Never one to quit, Sara Jane then went over to a new senior citizen volunteer who was not aware of the schedule, and she said "Sure." Persistence had paid off for Sara Jane.

HELP!

While Sara Jane's failure to accept the teacher's response to her request was a minor matter, it does help to illustrate a problem adults often have when dealing with children, and that is the lack of consistency. Behavior problems, especially those of a more serious nature, will be resolved much more readily if there is a consistent response from all the adults involved.

For the "You just know it is going to happen" event, develop a carefully thought-out game plan. Have in mind appropriate responses to the negative behavior before it occurs. Everyone involved should agree on how the situation will be handled. Consistency from all the adults in dealing with a recurring problem will make evaluating progress much easier.

When considering strategies, try to analyze what happens just before the negative event occurs. What, if anything, is causing the child to act up at this particular time?

- ☆ Is the child tired?
- ☆ Does she need more physical space?
- ☆ Does she need more time to transition between activities?

☆ Does she need to play with others?
☆ Does she need to play alone?
☆ Does she get too stimulated in large groups?

It can be any number of things and situations that set her off. Whatever the cause or suggested solution, the adults should present a unified approach to the recurring problem.

Keep in mind the child's usual pattern of behavior. If it is a single isolated event, it could be a one-time occurrence that deserves a pass. All human beings will occasionally have an off day. Coming down with a cold, having a restless night, or anxiety or excitement about an upcoming event will cause anyone to behave differently. If a normally cooperative, agreeable child misbehaves, give her the benefit of the doubt for the short term.

> We should explain the daily schedule to new volunteers and help them adjust to the classroom routine. While we want them to feel comfortable and free to interact with the children, they need to understand the importance of checking with other staff members before making any decisions that they are not sure about.

ASK YOURSELF:

Do you and the other adults work as a team, or do you send mixed signals to the children?

Do you regularly meet with the other adults in your classroom to discuss behavior management and discipline?

Is the approach to discipline consistent?

Do you explain the daily schedule and help new volunteers adjust to the classroom routine?

Do volunteers feel comfortable asking you for advice and guidance?

19. Give children positive attention

ANY ATTENTION IS BETTER THAN NO ATTENTION

Ms. Hugs, the teacher of the two-year-old class, was very upset. She had a biter in her class and felt things were getting worse and worse. There did not seem to be any pattern or time of day when the incidents occurred. Parents were starting to complain, and she was at her wits' end. I asked how she had handled it so far. She said that when an incident occurred she would take the child aside and reject the biting behavior. Sounded like good standard procedure to me. I offered to come observe the class. Maybe I could spot something that was causing this child to bite.

On Tuesday morning, I had some spare time and sat near the block corner to observe the children. Ms. Hugs was very involved with the art project, and Benjamin (the biter) was playing with some trucks. Noah came over and sat near Benjamin. Two minutes later Noah was howling, and we knew Benjamin had struck again. Ms. Hugs raced over, checked Noah, who was fine, and immediately turned her attention to Benjamin. She scooped him up, went out in the hallway and in gentle tones, while rocking her body with Benjamin still in her arms, explained that biting was not proper. Benjamin responded by listening carefully and stroking Ms. Hugs' hair.

Not wanting to jump prematurely to any conclusions, I decided to observe again on Wednesday. This time I sat in the book corner, and once again Ms. Hugs was very involved in the art project. Benjamin seemed unable to get involved in anything. He played with some beads, glanced at a book, and then after staring at Ms. Hugs, wandered over to Vanessa and took a bite out of her foot. Once again Ms. Hugs rushed over, all upset, checked Vanessa and then scooped up Benjamin and took him out into the hallway for a private conference.

I believe that when Benjamin was feeling lonely he would chomp on a limb of the nearest child since that would then guarantee him at least a five-minute private get-together with Ms. Hugs in the hallway.

HELP!

Occasionally, a child can become so desperate for attention that even negative attention is better than none at all. Ms. Hugs, by making such a dramatic issue of the biting incidents, and then bringing Benjamin out in the hallway for a private meeting, was in fact reinforcing the very behavior she was trying to stop.

Our strategy for the future was to try to give more positive attention to Benjamin before he took action himself. We also agreed that if he bit someone, the assistant teacher, not Ms. Hugs, would remove him to a quiet area in the room, and in clear simple language tell him, "You can bite a cookie or a carrot, but it is not okay to bite people. I will not let you bite people." Eventually, Benjamin did break the habit of biting for attention.

> Be careful not to have a knee-jerk reaction to a child's negative behavior. Try to understand why the child is behaving the way he is. You want an effective response, not one that inadvertently reinforces the negative behavior.

> When talking with a child about negative behavior, use short statements that are easy for the child to understand. If possible, offer positive alternatives, such as, "We talk to people; we do not hit."

ASK YOURSELF:

Do you try to give all the children enough positive attention so they do not resort to negative behavior in order to be noticed?

When rejecting a child's negative behavior, do you use short, easy-to-understand sentences?

20. Use tangible rewards sparingly

STICKERS AND GOLD STARS, OR, "WHAT WILL YOU PAY ME?"

I attended a workshop offered by a psychologist; the topic was behavior modification. Her perspective was based on the premise that everyone needs tangible rewards. She grabbed my attention by stating: "You go to work for paychecks. If there weren't any paychecks, there wouldn't be any teachers." I felt this was faulty logic. I was a teacher because I found it satisfying, stimulating, and enjoyable, not because of financial rewards.

The psychologist then explained that gold stars, stickers, and other little trinkets were very effective when used to motivate young children. They were presented as an easy fix to behavior problems with the young child. I have to say that over the years this line of reasoning has won many converts. Many parents and teachers have a huge supply of stickers and use them regularly. I fear they have not considered the long-term consequences of this approach.

HELP!

I cannot argue the fact that young children respond well to offers of treats, stickers, and gold stars. However, there is a serious downside to this approach to behavior modification that too many people are not aware of, or choose to ignore. This downside usually does not rear its ugly head until the child has moved on to grade school. That is when you get to pay the piper. Sooner or later the child realizes that he is being paid to clean up his room, do a chore or homework assignment, and then asks the question, "What will you give me to clean up my room?" Now Pandora's Box is open. As the sophistication of the child grows, he learns to negotiate, "One sticker is not enough to clean up my room. I want two or three." This can build to the point of outright bribery, and what started out as a reward system has the potential to become a blackmail scheme. Where does it end? Do the children ever learn that they have responsibilities, or are jobs and tasks viewed as just potential earning possibilities?

Reward and motivation must be very carefully considered. Verbal praise and acknowledgment are powerful tools that adults dealing with young children can and should use frequently. Tangible rewards, used sparingly and thoughtfully, should also be part of every child's life. However, we need to keep in mind that a sense of internal self-satisfaction for a job well done is an important trait to develop in a child. The satisfying feeling that comes from completing a task, caring for property, or solving a problem should be an inherent reward, not something based on external tokens.

Caring, respect, pride, and love are the best ways to motivate a child.

The reward of a thing well done is to have done it.

—Ralph Waldo Emerson

ASK YOURSELF:

Do you rely too heavily on cookies, treats, or the promise of bribes such as stickers or stars to influence the children's behavior?

21. Avoid power struggles

ON YOUR KNEES

It was time to leave the playground and go inside. Richard, a four-year-old, was at the farthest point from the classroom door and chose to stand his ground. He had on a few prior occasions waited for a special invitation to join us. Sometimes I would just ignore him, pretend not to notice that he wasn't with us, and he would then come running in at the last possible minute. This time I knew I would have to take the long walk across the playground to personally invite him inside.

When I reached him I said, "It is time to go in now." He smiled, and said, "No." I tried to cajole and lure him with various comments about the activities that were waiting inside, but that didn't work. I was now faced with the situation where, for safety reasons, I had no choice in the matter; it was definitely time to go in. Still trying to give Richard a face-saving way out of the situation, I said, "I can carry you inside like a baby, or you can walk inside like a big boy." Having played my last card, I was very disappointed to hear him again say, "NO." (I was feeling pretty stupid for having boxed myself into this situation, since he weighed about 40 pounds and I was in no mood to carry him clear across the playground.)

Fortunately, Richard came up with his own solution to the problem. He would not walk into the classroom as I requested, but he was willing to crawl on his knees to get there. While this sounded like a rather slow and uncomfortable method, did I really care how he moved to get into the classroom? My objective was just to get him inside. I said okay and turned to walk away. He dropped to his knees and began crawling. Poor kid, the blacktop was rough and crawling turned out to be very uncomfortable for him. Every now and then I could hear the pitter pat of his footsteps as he ran across the blacktop, but when I turned to check on his progress, he would again drop to his knees. Out of pity I stopped turning around so he could run most of the way back. I had what I wanted, Richard in the classroom, and he had (in addition to sore knees) his sense of pride at having contributed to the solution.

HELP!

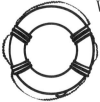 When faced with a power struggle, keep in mind what you are trying to accomplish. There are many ways to skin a cat. Try to offer the child a choice so he can feel as though he has some control over the situation and is not just obeying the adult. If a child suggests a solution that is reasonable and

meets your objectives, then you should be flexible and accept his ideas. Children need positive ways to assert their will, and this is a good opportunity for you to help them successfully work through and resolve a problem.

ASK YOURSELF:

Do you try to avoid power struggles by offering children choices?

Are you open to the child's solution, or do you just tell him what to do?

22. Quiet a group of screaming children by joining them

TO BEAT 'EM, JOIN 'EM

We had just finished cleaning up the room, and the children were gathering on the rug for story time. Sean and Hannah were filled with energy and started screaming as loud as they could—just for the fun of it. By the time I got across the room to the rug area, several children had joined in this playful game. I tried my best to tell them to use their indoor voices, and I gave as many un-approving looks as I was capable of. My efforts were having little if any effect. Judging from the noise level, the group seemed to be in chaos. (What would the neighbors think?)

Having failed to control the situation from the outside, I decided to join in the shout game. I too began to shout, and I made smiling eye contact with several of the children. Once I had infiltrated the enemy camp, I suggested we try a different sound, and made a popping noise. The children followed my lead, and after several different experiments with sounds, gradually lowering the volume as I progressed, I gained control of the situation and had them settle down for story time.

HELP!

With young children, spontaneous activities can sometimes become rowdy. It is more effective to join the group, become part of the shared activity, and then redirect it as you see fit, than to try to just shut it down cold. The screaming was a bit of exuberant fun, and sometimes it takes a little time before the children can be stopped or redirected. It is much safer and easier for you to be in the thick of it, rather than on the outside trying ineffectively to stop it.

Whispering is another way to get children's attention. Rather than always trying to talk above the roar, why not talk below it?

ASK YOURSELF:

Do you join a spontaneous activity and try to redirect it from within rather than trying to shut it down cold?

23. Redirect negative play

WHEN DEMAND EXCEEDS SUPPLY

The restaurant I had set up in the dramatic play area was a great hit. One could even say too great a hit. The competition to get a menu so you could order food was fierce and starting to become physical. There were just too many customers. I had clearly not prepared enough material. In a desperate attempt to remedy the problem of too many children and too few menus, I asked the children if they had money to pay the bill. Of course they did not. I then suggested that we go over to the art table and make some play money before we go to the restaurant. Several children thought this was a good idea and stayed with the money-making activity for a long period of time. Some created very respectable fortunes. (Ah, if only it were that easy in real life!)

This strategy of children making play money worked equally well for other dramatic play situations such as a pet store, going to the movies, and going shopping. (I'm embarrassed to say that a few children even tried to use the money to play cops and robbers.)

HELP!

 Redirecting children to other activities is a very effective technique and should not be limited to crowded dramatic play situations. It can and should be used in all parts of the classroom and on the playground. Rather than just saying "no" or stopping negative or too-rough play, we should offer suggestions and/or materials to children that will take their play in a more positive direction.

ASK YOURSELF:

Do you redirect negative play in a positive and non-confrontational way?

Do you make suggestions and offer children alternate ideas and/or materials?

24. Help children learn to take turns

I'M SORRY

Alexis was an assertive young lady. If there was a toy she wanted that was already in use, she did not hesitate to grab, shove, or punch a child to get it. However, it is only fair to report that while Alexis was willing to be violent, she was also extremely polite. In fact, just before grabbing a toy or hitting a child she would always look the child straight in the eye and with great conviction say, "I'm sorry." She then proceeded to clobber the poor victim.

HELP!

 Clearly Alexis needed to learn to take turns. One way to deal with this situation is to respond to the child's behavior by saying, "I know you want to play with the doll, but Jane is using it now." This shows her that you are an understanding adult and that you recognize and validate her desire for the doll. It also lets her know that others have needs too. You can then offer helpful redirection suggestions such as, "Why don't you play with the other doll while you wait for your turn?"

ASK YOURSELF:

Do you help children learn to take turns?

25. Don't overreact when children test your limits

HEAR NO EVIL

During circle time the following occurred:

Teacher:	Tomorrow is the big day. We will be going to the zoo. After we see the animals, we will have a picnic lunch.
First child:	I'm going to throw a meatball at you.
Teacher	(visibly upset at this remark): I don't think so; that isn't very nice.
Second child:	I'm going to throw a meatball at you, too!
Teacher:	(says nothing, but again shows anger on her face)
Third child:	I'm going to throw a meatball at you with tomato sauce on it.

Things just went downhill from there, with an angry teacher and a silly group of children.

HELP!

Children will use humor or nasty language as a way of testing limits. Four-year-olds are most proficient at this skill. Often I choose not to hear what is said, unless it becomes contagious (several other children join in), as it did in the above incident. I prefer, without missing a beat or showing any visible reaction, to continue with what I was going to say.

Do not give the child the power to interrupt and gain control of what you were planning on doing. Not hearing and, more important, not responding to children who are obviously trying to be confrontational can be a very effective strategy. As the adults, we have the power to pick and choose what we respond to. Let's choose wisely.

The teacher could have dealt with the situation in other ways:

☆ She could have turned the meatball comment into a positive by posing questions like, "Do you think they feed the animals at the zoo meatballs?" "Do you think bears like meatballs?" "What do you think the animals at the zoo like to eat?"

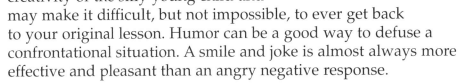

☆ She might have handled the situation with silly humor. The teacher could have said, "Make sure you have Parmesan cheese on my meatball." This, of course, opens you up to the creativity of the silly young child and may make it difficult, but not impossible, to ever get back to your original lesson. Humor can be a good way to defuse a confrontational situation. A smile and joke is almost always more effective and pleasant than an angry negative response.

If what has been said is so out of line that you feel you must respond, then stay very calm and reject the language. You could say, "I don't like to hear those words," using the same tone as if you were discussing whether or not you like cauliflower or broccoli. Often young children do not understand what they are saying. They are repeating something heard on TV or said by a big brother or sister. What they will understand is a dramatic response from an offended adult. Then, they realize they have something very powerful that can upset just about anyone, and they will be anxious to try out this newfound power frequently.

The art of being wise is the art of knowing what to overlook.

—William James

ASK YOURSELF:

Do you avoid overreacting to testing of limits or naughty language?

Do you think of ways to turn negative situations into positive ones?

26. Have developmentally appropriate expectations

SEE NO EVIL

During story time Yria was lying on the floor in the back of the group, quietly rocking herself. The other children were all sitting up, paying attention, and enjoying the story.

Teacher: Yria, please sit up.

Yria: (ignores the teacher and continues gently rocking herself)

Teacher: Yria, you really need to sit up like the rest of the children.

Yria: (continues to ignore the teacher. One or two children turn around to see what Yria is doing.)

Teacher (putting book down, repeats herself): Yria, you need to sit up now.

Yria: (continues rolling around, and now that the story has been interrupted and there is nothing else to look at, a few more children turn around to see just what Yria is doing)

Teacher: (picks up book and starts reading again)

Jack, having noticed what Yria is doing, decides that it looks like a lot of fun and joins her. Jack rolls around more vigorously and bumps into Carlos. Carlos decides the story is getting dull, what with all the interruptions, and he joins in the rolling game.

Teacher (slams the book closed): I guess we don't want to hear the rest of this story now.

HELP!

By talking to Yria, the teacher was drawing the children's attention away from the story. She was sabotaging her own lesson. Some children may not be developmentally ready to sit in a group situation. Allow them to play or sit quietly nearby. After a while, when the child is ready, she will come closer in order to see and hear what you are doing.

Don't assume a child is not paying attention just because she is not sitting bolt upright and staring you in the face. Some children with attention problems are able to pay *better* attention if they can fidget and squirm around a bit.

I remember the lesson a cute three-year-old taught me. During story time she fussed with an untied shoelace (in the good old days before Velcro, at least shoelaces were a quiet distraction). I was very disappointed that she had not paid attention. At snack time, she pleasantly surprised me when she enthusiastically joined in the conversation about the book. Children are capable of doing two things at once, like fuss with a shoelace and listen to a story.

ASK YOURSELF:

Do you have developmentally appropriate expectations of a young child's behavior, or do you expect absolute attention and obedience?

27. Limit the number of class rules

RULES

The Judeo-Christian tradition offers us the Ten Commandments and the Golden Rule as guides for good behavior. In Bolivia and Peru, based on ancient tradition, you are told in the daily greeting: "Do not be lazy, do not lie, and do not steal." That seems to cover most situations.

I am amused at the long lists of rules that teachers post in their classrooms. They are often so wordy and lengthy that the teacher cannot repeat them from memory. She has to go over to the chart and read the rules. Yet, some teachers seriously expect young children to remember what they themselves cannot.

HELP!

 To be effective, rules must be extremely simple and clear. Long lists of do's and don'ts, about everything from running to eating, can overwhelm young children. Very simple language and declarative statements such as, "Be gentle" or "Listen when someone talks" are more likely to have a chance of being remembered. I confess that I never posted a set of class rules.

ASK YOURSELF:

Do you have too many class rules for children to remember or live up to?

28. Help children deal with insults from other children

"YOU'RE STUPID"

Adam, a small and gentle three-year-old, was happily painting at the easel. He was experimenting by blending the dark blue paint with pale green. Walter walked by, paused for a moment to observe the painting, and with a flare of bravado said, "That is ugly." Adam had endured insults from Walter before, and this time he had been coached by his Mom to say, "I don't like it when you say those things. It hurts my feelings and makes me very sad." Walter looked at him, smiled broadly and said in a very confident loud voice, "It's ugly, and you're stupid." Score one for Walter.

HELP!

As sure as there is a verbal bully in every group, there is just as sure to be a victim. After trying insults on other children without getting satisfying results, the bully learns to target the victim with unerring accuracy each and every time. The poor child that becomes the victim will spend an eternity being teased and insulted by those who sense his weakness and inability to respond well.

While we must try to stop verbal attacks, we will not always be close enough to hear all the unkind things some children say. We need to assure the victims that the negative comments are not true. We also need to help the victims learn strategies to cope with the insults. For example:

- ☆ Tell the bully to STOP saying nasty things
- ☆ Ignore the insults
- ☆ Laugh at them
- ☆ Say they are silly
- ☆ Turn them into a joke

The verbal bully, not getting the satisfaction of a sad reaction, will then move on. There will always be verbally aggressive children who tease and taunt their classmates. In addition to stopping these verbal bullies, let's also try to make their potential victims more competent at handling the inevitable insults.

Violence of the tongue is very real—sharper than any knife.

—Mother Teresa

ASK YOURSELF:

Do you stop verbal bullying?

Do you teach potential victims skills and techniques so they can successfully deal with verbally aggressive children on their own?

29. Stop physical bullying

KARATE LESSONS

When my older son was in elementary school, he kept coming home with tales of being shoved and punched by a larger, stronger child when in the cloakroom and on the playground. After complaints about many such incidents, I requested a conference with his teacher. This was a person who had been teaching for over 20 years, and I respected her skill and experience. The bottom line of our meeting was that she said she couldn't be everywhere at once, and my son was going to have to learn to deal with it himself. She said that since he was small he was likely to be bullied again. She suggested that I have him take karate lessons.

HELP!

Physical bullying is a very serious problem that parents, teachers, and the community need to address. Together we must set firm limits for unacceptable behavior, and do everything possible to prevent children from being bullied. Victims cannot and should not have to protect themselves from physical violence. Asking the victim to handle the situation on his own or learn karate is not an acceptable solution.

ASK YOURSELF:

Do you set clear behavioral guidelines?

Do you stop physical bullying immediately?

Do you involve parents in an attempt to stop bullying behavior?

30. Don't assume the younger or smaller child is an innocent victim

THE TEASE MONSTER

My older son preferred quiet pursuits. He enjoyed board games, puzzles, and (a teacher's dream) he loved to read. His younger brother (by 18 months) was very sociable and active. He found it unbearable to be alone in a room. His greatest joys were wrestling and chase games. My sons always seemed to be arguing or, worse, punching one another. The usual scenario was that I would become aware of a disruption and then locate the older brother either chasing or sitting on top of the younger one and about to land a punch. Of course, I intervened and stopped the violence. Eventually I came to understand that whenever the younger child was a little bored he would scoot into his brother's room and do a little teasing jig, make faces, or do anything else that was sure to initiate a chase game.

I did the typical Mom thing. I asked the older child to be mature, set the example, and please just ignore the teasing. Somehow it always seemed to be the older brother's problem to resolve. Strange that I never noticed that while my older son was very unhappy and angry, the younger one, even though he was about to become a victim, was in fact enjoying himself.

Unfortunately, this teasing behavior was well learned and soon reared its ugly head at the school bus stop and in other locales.

HELP!

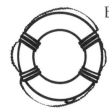 By holding my older son responsible for the fights, I had created a tease monster. My younger son learned that teasing was a fun game, there were few consequences, and if you picked on big kids, they would probably get the blame for the incident.

Clearly my younger son needed to learn more positive ways to engage children in play activities. In hindsight, which is 20–20, I am sorry I did not intervene on behalf of my older son more often.

> We should not always assume that the older/bigger child is responsible for altercations, or that he is the one who has to show self-control or be more understanding. It takes two to make a fight, and two to resolve the problems that cause fights.

ASK YOURSELF:

Do you usually assume that the younger or smaller child is an innocent victim?

Do you consider children who are older or physically larger to be responsible for problems and disputes?

31. Recognize tricks children use to gain favor

SING A SONG

Lara was a very appealing little girl. She had sparkly eyes and was basically agreeable. One day we were at the snack table, and Lara reached to the center of the table for one more piece of orange. As she did this, she knocked over her juice cup, spilling juice all over the table. In a beautiful clear voice, she immediately started singing a song about little baby Jesus. (I had never had a reaction to spilled juice quite like that before, or since.) When she finished her song, I assured her that people sometimes spill things, and I would help her clean it up.

The next day Lara grabbed a favorite doll away from a classmate. The classmate started to cry, and Lara started to sing again. It was quite a sight, one child crying and the other singing a hymn ever louder, trying to cover up the sound of the crying child. This pattern of behavior (when in trouble sing a religious song) was firmly entrenched. Fortunately, she had a lovely voice.

HELP!

Be aware of the little tricks that some children learn in order to deal with tough situations or angry adults. Hugs, cute smiles, bowed heads, crocodile tears, running away as fast as possible, and even singing songs may be part of their repertoire. They also learn that each adult is different, and what works with one adult may not work with another.

ASK YOURSELF:

Do you recognize the cute little tricks some children rely on to win over adults?

Do you carefully use discipline evenhandedly?

32. Be sure you have a child's undivided attention

DIVIDE TO CONQUER

Charles and Rob were buddies. They sat together, played together, and misbehaved together. On one occasion they had been very disruptive in the block corner, and I needed to have a serious discussion with them about safety, respecting property, and playing with other children. As I talked to Charles, he seemed to find my opinion very amusing (not the reaction I was hoping for). He was filled with bravado as he looked at Rob during my remarks. Not having much luck with Charles, I turned to Rob and didn't do any better. I then moved Rob to another, more private location and realized that once the visual contact with his buddy had been disrupted the dynamics changed. I now had his undivided attention, and the attitude that this was all a joke or a game disappeared. It was clear that I could be much more effective if the buddies did not have visual or verbal contact with one another.

HELP!

Sometimes children derive what I call negative strength from one another. They are more likely to challenge the adult with displays of bravado when they feel the support of a buddy. Quite often a joint conference to discuss an issue is very useful, but try to position the children in such a way that they do not get negative strength from visual contact with one another.

When having a serious discussion with a child, be aware of what is behind you that might distract the child. Try to position yourself so your back is to a wall and the child will have no distractions (or friends to entertain) while you are talking over important matters.

> Be careful not to handle discipline situations in too private an area. The other children usually realize something is wrong, and their imaginations can run wild wondering about what terrible things happen to a child who has been removed from the group.

ASK YOURSELF:

Do you carefully position yourself when talking to children to help ensure their undivided attention?

Do you remain in sight of the other children when dealing with discipline situations, keeping in mind that children can learn a lot from observing?

33. Help children learn to express anger and frustration without resorting to physical violence

FIGHTING MAD

Dick was happily playing with his favorite toy, a dump truck. Edward came over and tried to grab it away from Dick. This made Dick furious, and he started punching Edward. The teacher raced over to break up the fight.

HELP!

Often, when a child hits another child it is because of uncontrollable anger. He is very upset and feels it is the only thing he can do. It must be made clear to the child that while being upset is a valid human emotion, hitting is not acceptable.

Children need to learn how to protect themselves and express frustration and anger without resorting to physical violence. We need to help them learn to use words to express themselves. For example:

- ✯ Stop! Don't do that!
- ✯ Stop! I'm using the truck now. You can use it after me.
- ✯ I'm using it. You can get another truck.

ASK YOURSELF:

Do you help children learn how to use words to deal with anger and frustration?

34. Guide children through the problem-solving process

CRIME AND PUNISHMENT

After three-year-old Tyler crashed into a large block structure and caused blocks to go flying in all directions, I asked him to sit down for a moment and think about what he had just done. He replied meekly, "I can't do that." When I asked why not, he said, "My mother didn't teach me how to think yet."

HELP!

The purpose of discipline is to have a child change his behavior. Before he can do that, he must first learn to recognize unacceptable behavior and then understand how to change it. To help the child learn this skill we should ask him to think about what happened, and then guide him through the process of coming up with ideas on how to avoid such problems in the future. As part of this process we can ask the child such questions as:

- ✩ Are you happy or sad?
- ✩ Did something or someone make you angry?
- ✩ Do you want something?
- ✩ What is the problem?

After the child responds to the questions, give him some time to think of a solution. Then offer suggestions, provide explanations, and ask additional questions to help him solve the immediate problem and hopefully apply the technique to future problems as well.

- ✩ Is there a way to share the toy?
- ✩ If you want something, you can ask for it.
- ✩ When you hit, it hurts.
- ✩ If someone makes you angry, you need to tell them.
- ✩ Can you think of a way to solve the problem?
- ✩ Can you think of another way to solve the problem?

Giving children the opportunity to think through problems is an excellent approach, as long as it is done in a positive way, and we are careful to limit the time we have them spend thinking about what happened. A good rule of thumb is one minute for each year of age. Longer than that and the child's mind starts to wander, or he gets distracted and finds something else to do.

We need to make it very clear that while we reject the negative behavior we are not rejecting the child.

Remember, the use of discipline should be a learning experience for the child, not a show of adult power. Overwhelming a child with too severe or too long-lasting a punishment is not effective and teaches the child nothing positive. The old adage that the punishment should fit the crime is not applicable when dealing with young children.

Parents should be advised that sending a child to his room for a long period of time is often counterproductive. With toys, games, and books available, it can easily become just a change in location and activity, rather than an opportunity for reflection about behavior. The optimum time is just long enough for the child to be bored, but not so long that he becomes engaged in another activity.

The best discipline, maybe the only discipline that really works, is self-discipline.

—Walter Kiechel III

ASK YOURSELF:

Do you merely try to stop negative behavior, or do you guide children through a thinking process so they learn to recognize and modify unacceptable behavior?

Are you careful to reject the behavior but not the child?

Try This

Create an "emotional therapy box" for children to use when they are angry or upset but before they lose control. It should contain such things as:

☆ Play dough or clay
☆ Things to squeeze, like soft stuffed toys
☆ Things to throw, like beanbags and Nerf balls
☆ Things that are okay to bang hard, such as hammer and nails
☆ Paper to tear
☆ A drum to beat on

Encourage positive physical activity:

☆ Do exercises
☆ Provide a place and time where children can run fast, jump, and yell
☆ Have things to kick such as milk cartons, paper boxes, balls
☆ Provide a place to dig in the soil

Read books to children that deal with feelings, and then discuss them:

☆ *Alexander and the Terrible, Horrible, No Good, Very Bad Day* by Judith Viorst
☆ *Hands Are Not for Hitting* by Martine Agassi
☆ *Ira Sleeps Over* by Bernard Waber
☆ *Pierre* by Maurice Sendak
☆ *The Way I Feel* by James Cain
☆ *When Sophie Gets Angry—Really, Really Angry* by Molly Bang
☆ *Where the Wild Things Are* by Maurice Sendak

Use supportive positive language and alternatives to saying no:

☆ I like the way you share toys
☆ I like the way you are gentle with books

☆ You can run on the playground, but you can't run in the classroom
☆ You can roll the ball, but you can't throw it indoors
☆ You can bite the cracker, but you can't bite Jane
☆ John is using that toy; here's another one for you to use
☆ This book is for me; you can find one over there
☆ Kim is using the car; soon you can play with it; use the truck while you are waiting
☆ We don't hit; we touch gently

"Will You Be My Friend?"

Helping Children Develop a Positive Self-Image and Master the Art of Getting Along With Others

So much in life depends on our own self-image and how we get along with others. To be successful we must have the ability to relate well to people. Children need to have interpersonal experiences in order to develop the social skills they will require to function successfully as adults in the business world, personal relationships, and society in general.

We must all learn to live together as brothers.
Or we will all perish together as fools.

—Martin Luther King, Jr.

35. Foster a positive self-image

I CAN'T DO THAT

Three-year-old Terry would come into school and stand around until someone came over, unbuttoned her coat, and helped her take it off. When it was time to go outside she was overwhelmed with the thought of having to put on a jacket. She made no attempt to do it herself, but instead just waited around until some adult would lend assistance. While the coat business was not serious, it was indicative of an "I can't do anything" mental attitude. This reliance on adults extended to the bathroom where Terry would sit on the seat calling out, "Someone come wipe me."
I responded to Terry's call by suggesting that she do it herself. "I can't do that. Granny says I'm too small," she responded. A look of amazement came over her when I challenged her remark and said, "I think you're a big girl. You can do it yourself." Terry was delighted with that statement. She managed the task at hand. I encouraged her to tell Granny that she was a big girl now and could do things herself.

HELP!

 Terry came from a troubled family. Mom and Dad were in the process of getting a divorce, and Grandma was raising Terry while Mom was at work trying to earn enough money to keep food on the table.

In an understandable attempt to shower the grandchild with attention and loving care, the grandmother was inadvertently having a negative effect. Terry was developing a very poor self-image, and thought she was too incompetent to do anything. This extra dose of care was ruining her self-confidence.

Children who have a poor self-image and feel incompetent develop a defeatist attitude. They must be encouraged to try new tasks, and be willing to risk failure on occasion, in order to grow and flourish. The second grader who says, "I can't read, I can't do math, I can't . . ." learned an attitude of failure and incompetence from somewhere. We need to be careful that we don't create quitters.

Support children, show confidence in their abilities, and if they fail, let them know it is okay, they just need to try again.

It is hard to fail but it is worse never to have tried to succeed.

—Teddy Roosevelt

ASK YOURSELF:

Do you try to foster a positive self-image in children by encouraging them to be as independent as their skill level permits?

Do you treat failure as a normal occurrence that happens to everyone, and teach children not to let it discourage them?

36. Caution parents about the dangers of being too indulgent

A ROYAL PRINCESS

Xiao Chen was raised on a small farm in China. She shared some interesting observations with me about her homeland. "Capitalism has come to China in a big way. Some people say money is the new god." She also commented on the impact of the government's policy to limit families to just one child. She told stories of children who never have to share toys or a parent's lap with a brother or sister. These children never have to be quiet because the baby is sleeping, never have to wait for a brother to be ready before going out to play, never have to negotiate to decide who sits where at the kitchen table or what TV show to watch. They do not have to learn to take turns and are constantly given treats by doting grandparents. I wonder what these children will be like when they grow up. It will be interesting to see what the policy of one child per family will have on the social fabric of Chinese society.

HELP!

One does not have to be the parent of an only child or financially well off to be guilty of spoiling a child. Parental behavior that consists of being too indulgent, not setting limits, rarely saying "no" to a child's requests, or never requiring her to delay gratification can cause the child to develop a distorted sense of entitlement. Overly permissive parents can negatively impact a child's future ability to function successfully with others in society. In an article discussing what happens to kids developmentally and emotionally who have everything they want, psychologist Mary Pipher says, "They're set up to be narcissistic, spoiled, not inclined to work hard, and with impulse-control problems."

How children are treated in their early years will have an effect on their future relationships with supervisors, coworkers, friends, peers, and mates. We need to help parents understand that if they treat a child like a princess, she may grow up with an unrealistic image of her place in society. The rest of the world may not be as willing to pay homage to her royal highness.

ASK YOURSELF:

Do you counsel parents on the serious negative effects of being overly indulgent and not setting limits?

37. Find something positive to say about each child

HORSE SENSE

Whenever I had an idea or suggestion my mother would smile broadly and say to me, "See, you have horse sense." Not exactly the attribute I wanted to brag about to friends and neighbors, but privately her opinion of my special talent served me very well. I tried to live up to her perception of me, and worked hard to think of new and better ways to do things. My reward of a big smile from my Mom and a "See I told you so, you have good horse sense" was always treasured. I came to believe I could be successful and do well in school or anywhere as long as I approached things with old-fashioned horse sense.

HELP!

It makes all the difference in the world when a child feels good about herself. In every child we should find positive things that we can acknowledge and support with regularity. Highlight some positive attributes that she can cling to and develop. It could be such things as, "You are thoughtful, smart, persistent, generous, considerate, friendly, or always nice to be with." Having horse sense is good too, but I would like to suggest calling it common sense.

Children develop their self-image from the feedback they get from the adults they come in contact with. If adults thoughtlessly laugh at a child or say negative things like, "You're just dumb, bad, or [the one I dislike the most] no good," the child will eventually come to believe the label. She will define herself as bad or dumb and start to live up to the negative label. Who can blame her? After all, it is what Mom, Dad, or her older brothers and sisters say to her all the time. By talking negatively about the child they wind up unintentionally reinforcing the very traits they thought they were rejecting.

Kind words can be short and easy to speak, but their echoes are truly endless.

—Mother Teresa

ASK YOURSELF:

Do you find something positive to reinforce in each child?

Do you avoid using negative labels?

38. Provide activities that involve cooperation

GETTING TO KNOW YOU

I can still remember going to Girl Scout camp all by myself. I was terrified. I did not have a friend or even know someone to talk to.

As adults you probably have gone to a social event or meeting where you knew only a few people and hunted them down as your first priority upon arriving. Even for adults, being alone with strangers can be awkward and stressful.

HELP!

In the beginning of the school year try as soon as possible to help the children interact with one another. As part of my first music lesson, I do a jumping song. Then I tell the children to jump holding hands with someone else. There is no better way to get young children to interact than giggling and jumping around together. I do the song several times, asking the children to select different partners to be with each time.

Other opportunities for cooperative interaction are:

☆ Have children pretend to be rowboats with partners for the song "Row, Row, Row Your Boat."

☆ When doing the song/finger play "Eency Weency Spider," have each child provide one hand to do the spider movement.

☆ In the following finger play about a bunny that jumps down a hole, have one child use his fingers to be the bunny and the other child use her fist to make the hole.

> Here's a bunny with ears so funny
> (Hold up two fingers to make bunny ears)
> And this is his hole in the ground
> (Make a hole with fingers of other hand)
> At the first sound he hears, he wiggles his ears
> And then hops into his hole in the ground
> (Use motion of bunny jumping into a hole)

Provide activities throughout the day that help children learn to work together cooperatively. We should not limit ourselves to doing these types of activities only in the beginning of the school year. They are important, and we should do them often throughout the year.

ASK YOURSELF:

Do you provide cooperative play activities all year long?

39. Encourage the children to interact positively with all their classmates

PLAY WITH ME

In the beginning of the school year, four-year-old Connie spent most of her time happily interacting with other children in the dramatic play corner or at the art table. Alice, who joined the class in November, also enjoyed dramatic play and art activities. It is logical to think that interaction between Connie and Alice was inevitable, but it wasn't. As a matter of fact, Connie would promptly leave any activity as soon as Alice approached. Connie started to spend an unusual amount of time sitting by herself looking at books. Her behavior seems hard to understand, until I mention the fact that Alice was confined to a wheelchair.

HELP!

 It is not unusual for young children to feel awkward or even afraid of dealing with children who have special needs. They often have irrational fears and misconceptions about these children, the challenges they face and the equipment that they use. These issues need to be addressed, and opportunities for positive interaction arranged. Mainstreaming presents a good learning opportunity for both the child who has special needs and all the others in the classroom. With proper guidance, children can learn to be accepting, caring, and helpful.

- ♦ The teacher's role is crucial. She is the role model. Through her actions and words the children in the class will come to accept the child who has special needs.

- ♦ Children who have special needs should be encouraged to participate in all classroom activities to the best of their ability.

- ♦ Encourage children to accept the child who has special needs as an equal—someone whom they can help but should not treat like a baby.

ASK YOURSELF:

Do you role model acceptance of the child who has special needs?

Do you address the children's natural curiosity about children who have special needs and the equipment they use?

Do you help children get to know and interact with all their classmates, rather than just a few of them?

40. Arrange opportunities for children to help one another

SNOW GEAR

While I consider myself somewhat of an expert on zipping zippers and putting on boots, I still find getting a group of young children suited up for winter outdoor activities a major chore. It is not unusual to spend as much time getting the children into their ski pants, boots, coats, hats, and mittens as they actually spend outdoors playing. Other than putting on gloves, for me the two greatest challenges are:

1. To convince children that it is in fact easier to zip zippers or button coats BEFORE putting on their mittens.

2. Struggling to get the boots on a child who seems to have legs made of spaghetti, while simultaneously trying to keep the child who is completely suited up from getting into mischief. It always seemed unjust to me that the children who hardly have the self-control to sit on a chair somehow have the motor control to don hats, boots, and jackets in the wink of an eye.

HELP!

 Rather than having the early dressers just sitting around waiting for the others, challenge them to be helpers. Ask the children with the skill to put on boots or fasten zippers and buttons to help the other children get dressed.

This is a good social experience. Think about just how much cooperation is involved in getting a boot on someone else's foot. The child who needs help learns to seek as well as accept it from peers. The child with the skill learns how to offer help and gets to use the skill in a positive way. The responsibility and pleasure of helping others is a wonderful social lesson. However, I expect you will still need to remind everyone that mittens are the last thing we put on before walking out the door.

ASK YOURSELF:

 Do you arrange for situations where children can help one another?

Do you encourage children who can do something to help those who can't?

41. When developmentally appropriate, provide an atmosphere that encourages sharing

IT'S MINE!

The water table in the two-year-old class had become a battle zone. Crying, shoving, and a tug-of-war between Olivia and Kobe over the one and only pitcher was not something the teacher had anticipated. Water table activity usually has a calming effect on young children, but that was definitely not the case this day.

HELP!

Anyone who deals with children under the age of three should quickly realize that sharing is just about impossible for them. After all, the credo of a two-year-old is, "It's mine, mine, mine!" They believe that anything they see or touch is theirs. Therefore, try not to ask the impossible of them. While a large pitcher is a good item for a water table, if you do not have several of them, it can create a problem. A generous supply of cups and spoons would be better. When dealing with the very young child, we must be sure there are enough materials on hand for everyone to feel satisfied, or we run the risk of having a lot of unhappy children who are grabbing and arguing over equipment.

Once past this stage, children can and should learn to share. When the children are developmentally ready, think about ways to provide an atmosphere that encourages sharing:

☆ When doing a project involving paste in a four-year-old class, do not put out a portion of paste for each child. Put out half as many as you think they will need, and encourage the children to share the paste.

☆ You can also encourage sharing when using play dough. When a child joins the group already at the table, ask for volunteers to share with the new child. Some will give miniscule portions (it is all they can manage at this point), but fortunately there will usually be a few who are more generous. Of course, as the adult you should heartily and very publicly approve of how nicely they are sharing. (For emergency circumstances keep some play dough in reserve just in case you run into a group of cheapskates.)

ASK YOURSELF:

Do you provide a generous amount of material when dealing with two-year-olds?

Do you have developmentally appropriate expectations regarding a child's ability to share?

Do you, when developmentally appropriate, provide an atmosphere that encourages sharing?

42. Be a positive role model

ROUGH-AND-TUMBLE LOVE

Joey a short, stocky three-year-old, just loved to wrestle. Whenever Joey wanted to play with the other children he would tackle them to the ground. He always had an engaging smile, even when he appeared to be attacking the other boys in the class. Unfortunately for Joey, the other children did not interpret this as a friendly gesture. They soon grew tired of being knocked about and hurt, and I was tired of it as well. The children gave Joey a wide berth and avoided playing with him.

HELP!

As I chatted about this situation with Joey's mother, she became rather upset. She could not understand this behavior; he was such a smiley, loving little guy. I asked her how she showed affection to her son, and she said that she would hug, kiss, and hold hands. I then asked how Dad showed affection to Joey. The question caught her by surprise, but her answer was key. Dad was "a man's man." Joey already knew all about baseball, basketball, and football. She said Dad was very affectionate with Joey; they were always rolling around on the floor and playfully wrestling together. I asked if Dad ever touched Joey in a gentle way. The answer was no. It seemed that in Dad's scheme of things it was okay for a man to kiss or hug a woman; however, men could do only rough-and-tumble play to show affection to other males. No wonder Joey was so busy tackling all his peers. That was his role model.

Children observe and model behavior patterns. How adults relate to others, resolve disputes, deal with stress, and show respect and affection are all being closely observed.

Example is not the main thing in influencing; it's the only thing.

—Albert Schweitzer

ASK YOURSELF:

Are you a positive role model?

Do you keep in mind the fact that children are always observing you and your interactions with parents, staff members, and other children?

43. Give children the opportunity to resolve disagreements by themselves

PLAYING REFEREE

As a youngster I played stickball on Willoughby Avenue in Brooklyn. The ball field was the middle of the street. One sewer cover served as home plate, the next one down the street was second base. The tires on cars parked halfway between home plate and second base served as first and third base. We played our game as traffic allowed. When the light was red we could get a few players up at bat, when the light turned green we had to abandon the field and wait for the next traffic light cycle.

Choosing the captains for each team was the first order of business. One of the captains was usually the person who owned the ball and stick that we used as a bat. The other team captain was selected by playing "one potato-two potato" or flipping a coin.

Once the game got started there were frequent disputes over judgment calls that needed to be made:

Was the ball fair or foul?

Was Joe safe at first or out?

Was the ball hit long enough (out of the ball park) to be a home run?

Some of the lessons learned as a result of the way we resolved our disputes were:

☆ The owner of the ball said, "It's my ball and I'm safe or I'm going home and taking my ball with me." (There is power in ownership.)

☆ An older, bigger guy would yell loudly, "I was safe" while making a fist with a threatening gesture. (There are bullies.)

☆ Sometimes a group of three or four would band together to take a position against one of the bullies. (There is strength in numbers.)

If all this bickering did not resolve the conflict, there was always the option of a "do-over" or of flipping a coin. We all understood that playing the game was what we really wanted to do, and we would work out whatever problems arose in order to continue the game. While I didn't realize it at the time, Willoughby Avenue stick ball games provided an incredible learning opportunity in social dynamics.

HELP!

I encourage children, as much as possible, to learn how to resolve their problems on their own. If the children are reasonably satisfied with the outcome, I do not interfere. I try to avoid playing referee. By personally experiencing these give-and-take situations, and living with the results of their dispute resolution skills, children learn to deal with others.

> Adults who rush in too quickly to resolve a disagreement deprive children of the opportunity to develop critically important interpersonal skills.

ASK YOURSELF:

Do you step in to resolve disagreements prematurely, or do you monitor the situation and allow children to try and resolve their disagreements on their own?

44. Provide materials that encourage positive social interaction on the playground

GIVE ME A LIFT?

One of the most popular activities on the playground is going for a ride in the wagon. When children sit cramped together in a wagon and wait to be pulled, all sorts of negotiations are involved in the seating arrangements, as well as who will be strong enough to pull the wagon. If the load is too heavy someone has to volunteer to get off, or the children may eventually figure out that someone can push from the back while at the same time someone else pulls the handle at the front of the wagon. A great deal of coordination and cooperation is involved in just getting the wagon to move at all.

HELP!

Staff members should not be too willing to pull the wagon and give rides. Yes, sometimes we should join in, but after a while we should encourage the children to work together to give one another rides and to take turns as passengers or pullers. Of course, there are some children who always want to be the passenger, and sit there like a prince or princess, but after a few turns the pullers usually just walk away. They leave the passenger stranded, thereby providing a good object lesson about taking turns.

When purchasing outdoor equipment try to choose a few things that foster cooperative play. I think wagons or tricycles with platforms for passengers are much better choices than individual tricycles.

To create opportunities for cooperative interaction outdoors you can provide a few props to foster dramatic play. Have items available to suggest:

   ☆ A car wash
   ☆ Garage
   ☆ Gas station
   ☆ Toll booth
   ☆ Café

- ✩ Airplane
- ✩ Bus or train station
- ✩ Delivery truck
- ✩ Fast food restaurant drive-through window

ASK YOURSELF:

Do you provide materials on the playground that encourage positive social interaction and cooperation?

Do you pull the wagon filled with children, or do you encourage children to cooperate and pull it themselves?

45. Stimulate but do not dominate dramatic play

KNOW WHEN TO LEAVE

Ms. Hollywood, teacher of the three-year-old class, loved dramatic play. You could usually find her sitting in the housekeeping area. She would always attract a large group of children who busily prepared her favorite food, or otherwise followed her directions. They would go on pretend trips, have weddings, and always appeared to be having a great deal of fun. The participation was high, and dramatic play seemed to be a great success when she was there.

HELP!

Good teachers are like magnets. Wherever they go in the classroom, children follow. The wise teacher uses this natural magnetism to attract children and then help them get started in activities. By role modeling in dramatic play, we can suggest to the children some of the possibilities they might explore. However, if the teacher overstays her visit she will wind up directing and dominating the play.

The adult should stimulate an interest and then gracefully fade out of the picture so the children have the opportunity to explore and flourish. The best learning occurs when the children are left on their own. That is when the children's ideas will come forward.

Dramatic play teaches many things beyond vocabulary and some facts about a pretend post office or supermarket. This is where the children really learn social skills and how to deal with their peers. Compromise, leadership, accepting the ideas of others, or walking away from something you don't like or can't control are all experiences that children can grapple with during dramatic play. The best place to hone social skills is in the dramatic play area.

You should not spend all of your time interacting with the children. Stepping back and observing is also an important part of a teacher's job. You can learn a lot just by watching. Regular, frequent observations will help you identify the developmental level of each child, as well as his interests, strengths, and weaknesses. You should then use this knowledge to develop your lesson plans.

ASK YOURSELF:

Do you dominate and control dramatic play by your presence?

Do you withdraw as soon as possible from the activity so the children can play independently?

Do you encourage dramatic play as a way for children to develop social skills?

Do you regularly spend time observing the children so you can assess their progress, and prepare lesson plans to fit their needs and developmental levels?

46. Give children the privacy and freedom they need for dramatic play

I'M GOING TO BE A MOMMY

Our class had spent the last several days talking about doctors. The children had stethoscopes, X rays, facemasks, bandages, and other materials to use in their dramatic play. In all my years of working with young children, the following happened only once, and once was probably enough for me.

Julie, a four-year-old, could almost always be found in the dramatic play area. Her favorite ensemble, which she put on over her clothes, was a bright red lace and satin floor-length dress with matching high-heeled shoes and all the jewelry her little body could carry. One day as Julie was playing with one of the dolls she lifted up the red dress, placed the doll on her stomach, and then pulled the dress down and declared that she was going to be a Mommy. Later, Billy came over and noticed the bulge under the dress. He asked, "What's that?" Julie explained she was going to be a Mommy. Billy asked if he could be the doctor. Julie agreed and promptly lay down on the carpet. Billy carefully lifted the dress, removed the doll, considerately pulled the dress down and presented the doll to Julie. This game became all the rage, and soon I had five or six pregnant-looking four-year-olds wandering around my classroom and a shortage of dolls. The director wanted to know just what I was teaching.

HELP!

I'm sure it will come as no surprise to you that Julie's mother was pregnant. Julie was using dramatic play to try to understand what was happening in her life. Dramatic play can help children work through important issues and understand more about themselves and life in general. We should be sure to provide an environment that gives children both the privacy and the freedom to explore through dramatic play.

- ◆ Be sure the dramatic play area has a large safety (shatterproof) mirror for the children to use.

ASK YOURSELF:

Do you encourage the use of dramatic play to help children work through their concerns and ideas about the world?

Do you give children the privacy and freedom they need for dramatic play?

Do you maintain a nonjudgmental attitude about the children's dramatic play?

Try This

Design cooperative projects, such as:

- ☆ Painting a large box
- ☆ Painting or decorating a large mural
- ☆ Decorating a stage for puppets
- ☆ Building a totem pole made out of containers that each child has decorated
- ☆ Preparing food
- ☆ Fixing up the room for a holiday
- ☆ Planning a picnic

Do cooperative projects on the playground:

- ☆ Build a snowman
- ☆ Make a big pile of leaves
- ☆ Make a leaf man
- ☆ Dig a big hole
- ☆ Clean up the playground
- ☆ Plant a garden
- ☆ Make a scarecrow

Do cooperative movement activities, such as having two children walk from one location to another:

- ☆ Holding one hand facing forward
- ☆ Holding two hands facing each other
- ☆ Holding two hands back to back
- ☆ With a large pillow between them and their hands behind their backs
- ☆ Carrying a cup filled with water on a tray

Part II

Creating Positive Teacher-Family Relationships

"Mommy, Please Don't Leave Me!"

Preparing Parents and Children for School

September is one of my favorite months. The hot, dog days of summer are over. The air is usually crisp and clear, and you can stay on the playground forever. As a teacher, I look forward to new students, new families, and perhaps a new classroom or new furniture arrangement. All these things, which give me a sense of optimism, can be troubling to parents. They are filled with doubt: "Will my child have friends? Will she like the new teacher? What will she learn? Will things work as well as last year?" Of course, for the first school or separation experience, the questions and concerns are even more deeply felt. We must help the parents and the children get off to a good start IN THE BEGINNING.

47. Offer parents specific and concrete advice on how to minimize separation problems before the child enters school

CARING SOCIETY

As I drove my car I heard the following commercial on the radio. A woman with a sad, gentle voice said, "Mommy has to go to work now, be a good boy." This was followed by the sound of a dog whining. Then the announcer spoke: "Separation can cause anxiety; it can lead to negative behavior and acts of defiance. Call your veterinarian now for a behavior appointment."

After hearing this, I thought someone should run a similar commercial about young children. It is perfectly normal for children starting school to experience separation anxiety. Unfortunately, some parents, once they decide they are going to use child care, develop a defensive shell and a tough-it-out attitude. They believe their child will just have to adjust on his own.

HELP!

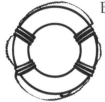 Before the children start school, you should prepare a letter with helpful hints to ease the trauma of separation. As a minimum, it could include the following suggestions:

* ✮ Use the teacher's name at home in a positive way to show your confidence in her and the program. For example, "Gwen likes to play outside. She has a nice smile. I know she helps the children a lot. She reminds me of our cousin Jane. I like her."

* ✮ Talk about some of the children in your child's class, using their names.

* ✮ Talk about school, for example, paint, play dough, toys, juice and crackers.

* ✮ Bring your child to school for a visit to meet the children and teachers.

☆ Tell your child where you will be and what you will be doing while he is at school.

☆ Let your child know you will miss him. This is an honest emotion that we should not deny.

☆ Send a favorite cuddly toy or blanket to school with your child. It can be very comforting.

☆ Do your very best to be on time to take your child home.

ASK YOURSELF:

Do you offer the parents specific and concrete advice on how to help their child and family make a smooth adjustment to school BEFORE the child starts school?

Do you recognize that parent/child separation can be traumatic?

48. Try to meet and form bonds with parents before school starts

WHOSE SEPARATION PROBLEM IS IT?

Before school started Mrs. J asked if she could stay in the classroom to be sure her daughter adjusted well. She went on to explain that there had been a lot of dramatic changes in the family's life recently, and she was worried about Sandy's adjustment to school. They had just moved here from out of state. Dad was in a new job. She had given birth to a son last month, and the kitchen in their new home was being completely renovated. That sounded like plenty of stress to me. The mother needed some TLC. I agreed to let her stay until her daughter adjusted.

Sandy, the cutest little two-year-old, came to school wearing a tool belt and pretending to fix everything in sight. She adjusted to the class routine with great ease and confidence. Mom was the one with the anxiety. After a few days of observing our caring, professional staff, Mom relaxed and comfortably left Sandy with us. (I think the fact that the electricity was back on in her kitchen also helped.)

HELP!

We should not make the mistake of underestimating the stress that parent-child separation puts on the adult. When adults feel comfortable about the school, staff, and program, they will be relaxed. When the parents have doubts and concerns, they communicate their uneasiness to their child, and the child will have a much harder adjustment period.

- ♦ You should have an orientation meeting with parents before school starts to explain what to expect, and how to deal with separation anxiety. Try to form bonds with the parents. Explain that you will be happy to tie shoelaces, wipe drippy noses, comfort an unhappy child, change wet pants, and generally care for the child in every way possible. This is what parents want and deserve to hear.

- ♦ If possible, try to arrange home visits to help you bond with the children before they come to school.

ASK YOURSELF:

Do you try to form bonds with parents before their child enters school?

Do you arrange to personally meet or at least talk by phone with the parents?

Do you treat each child and family as unique?

Do you try to reassure everyone of your commitment to helping them through any separation problems that may arise?

49. Establish good lines of communication with parents

BELIEVE ONLY HALF OF WHAT YOU HEAR

Danny had been in my four-year-old class for six months. He was a gentle contented soul. I don't ever remember his getting upset, fighting, or even raising his voice to the other children. His mother, Ellen, was most cooperative, always ready to come in to lend support for class projects or events. Bob, the father, had a hobby of rock collecting and shared many of his treasures with the children. They had two younger sons at home, both adopted and from racially mixed parents. Ellen was white, and Bob was African American.

One day Danny came to school and started relating a troubling story to the student teacher. He told her about Grandma who "didn't like black children, and kicked Nancy down the stairs." As he spoke he became very upset. "There was a lot of shouting and fighting. The little girl was hurt, and the mother had to go to the doctor because her arm was busted." I could see that the student teacher was visibly shaken and guessed she was jumping to the conclusion that Danny was talking about an incident that had happened at his home. I asked Danny if he had watched TV last night. He said, "Yeah, that show had a really mean Grandma."

I knew that Danny's grandparents had passed away years ago, and he did not have a sister. The story he had related was the plot of a TV show that I had seen the night before. It was on from 9 p.m. to 10 p.m., very dramatic, but clearly not appropriate for Danny to be watching at his age.

HELP!

To avoid problems and misunderstandings, families and teachers need to keep the lines of communication open and active. I conclude my parent orientation meeting with the following comments: "Reality and fiction can easily blur in the minds of young children. We as teachers and you as parents must remember that fact. Let's be sure to communicate with one another and not jump to conclusions about something that a young child says about school or life at home."

Child abuse is a very serious matter. Reporting suspected child abuse is required by law. It must be addressed promptly and carefully. Do not ask questions of parents or attempt to deal with a suspected problem on your own. If you have concerns, contact the agency in your community that is responsible for children's protective services for advice on how to proceed.

ASK YOURSELF:

Do you try to establish and maintain good lines of communication with parents?

Do you know what agency to contact for guidance if you have concerns about child abuse or neglect?

50. Help parents develop an exit strategy

DISAPPEARING ACT

Most children when told "Mommy [or Daddy] has to leave now" will inevitably put up a fuss. Obviously, the level of fuss varies considerably depending on the child and his age. Parents can be overwhelmed and embarrassed by a tortured scene of departure. They get flustered and do not know how to respond. Sometimes, in a misguided attempt to avoid creating a scene, parents will try to make a quick exit when their child is not looking. We all know that eventually the child realizes that Mommy or Daddy is gone. Since there was no official good-bye, the child may become panic stricken about his parents. He does not understand what happened to them.

As a result of this experience at school, the child's sense of trust may be affected. At a doctor's office, supermarket, or when visiting a friend's house, if the parent is not clearly in sight the child may jump to the conclusion that he has been abandoned.

HELP!

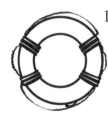

Parents should be offered help devising a smooth departure strategy from school. They need to be cautioned about the downside of leaving without saying goodbye. Encourage them to use reassuring words like, "Mommy will be back after nap time," or "when it gets dark out."

♦ Remember, saying "Mommy will be back soon" is open to different interpretations. The adult "soon" is not even close to the child's understanding of soon (which is usually under 60 seconds).

♦ Young children find comfort in routines. The following are some things that parents can do as part of a smooth exit strategy:

Do a puzzle together before leaving

Read one book before leaving

Develop a special hug or kiss routine, for example, a kiss on each cheek and then one on the nose

Give a high-five handshake

♦ Advise the parents that as they are leaving they need to communicate to the child through their words and body language that they are confident the child will have a good day and be well cared for at school.

ASK YOURSELF:

Do you help parents develop an exit strategy that does not include tricking the child to avoid a scene?

51. Encourage parents to stay nearby

JUMPING, BUT NOT FOR JOY

During the first week of school Pam, the assistant teacher, was trying to comfort Marissa, an unhappy two-year-old, when she got an uneasy feeling that she was being watched. She glanced over to the window and saw Mrs. Peek's face (Marissa's mother) appear, and then disappear. She continued looking for another few seconds and the face appeared again and then quickly disappeared. It was almost as though Mrs. Peek were jumping on a trampoline. Not sure what was going on, Pam turned to the teacher and asked her to look out the window. Sure enough, after about 10 seconds Mrs. Peek appeared for an instant and then disappeared. Poor Mrs. Peek, she would leave school and scurry around to the back of the building to look in the window of her daughter's classroom. The ground was sloped, and she would literally have to jump up and down to try to catch a glimpse of her two-year-old.

I have witnessed parents bravely leave their crying child, get in their car, and break down in tears. The sound of their child's cries will echo in their heads for hours.

HELP!

As teachers, we know that usually within five minutes after the parent is gone, the child settles in, bonds with the other adults, and gets involved in the activities of the day. To help put the mother's mind at ease, encourage her to wait for five minutes in another room or a nearby hallway (that is out of her child's sight). Not having to listen to her child crying as the last sound she hears before she goes off for her day means a great deal.

> Another way to ease parental anxiety is to videotape their child five minutes after they have left, so that they can see for themselves that the departure trauma is short lived.

Most children will make the adjustment to preschool or child care in a few weeks. In a good program, children will be disappointed when they cannot go to school on Saturday and Sunday. If a child or infant CONSISTENTLY becomes agitated or very upset when brought to a program, or is very anxious to go home at the end of the day, it is a warning sign. Remember that even infants can communicate through their body language, and we need to be sensitive to what they are saying. Parents may need some guidance about reevaluating the number of hours their child is in the program or even consider postponing their child's enrollment for a few months.

ASK YOURSELF:

Do you encourage parents to stay nearby, but out of sight, until their child has settled in?

Do you keep parents informed about any problems their child may be having?

52. Gradually increase
the time a child stays at school

LET ME OFF

Recently I was on a flight in Canada. AFTER we were airborne, the pilot made an announcement: "We will be landing at a small airport near the town of Iqaluit to refuel. It is snowing there, and the airport has a gravel runway. Our plane is equipped to land on gravel." I was rather upset with the news and not very reassured by the commentary, but the reality was that I had no choice—the pilot was in charge and I had to go along for the ride.

HELP!

As adults we can usually pick ourselves up and leave a bad movie, restaurant, party, or even job. We know we aren't really trapped in a situation (unless of course you are in a plane 30,000 feet in the air). But young children almost always have to go along for the ride. They have no way out. We must remember this perspective and be particularly sensitive to their concerns when they are starting school. They may be feeling trapped and panicky, and we must make the effort to reassure and comfort them as they adjust to new people and a new environment.

♦ One way to ease the adjustment to school is to arrange a schedule of gradually increased time for the children to be in the new situation. An hour or two may be all that they can handle for the first few days.

♦ In the beginning of the year, inviting half the group on alternating days is another effective way to ease the children into the new school experience.

It is far better for children to leave school with a smile on their face, eager to come back for more, than to have them stay too long and become reluctant to return in the future.

Advise parents to try to arrange their calendar so that they can be available for the first two weeks should their child encounter any difficulties and need a little extra support. It will make life much easier on them and their child.

ASK YOURSELF:

Do you arrange a schedule that gradually increases the time the children spend at school to help make their adjustment to the program easier?

53. Give all the children extra attention

LOOK, MA, NO TEARS

Raymond, a three-year-old, was simply amazing. On the very first day of school he walked boldly into the classroom, turned around and told his mother she needed to go now. The mother offered to stay a while, but Raymond insisted she leave and actually physically pushed her out the door. He then went over to the table and spent his time contentedly using the Magic Markers. It was unbelievable. I had my hands full with criers, clingers, and frightened children, and was grateful for this one easy child.

The following week, I noticed Raymond open the classroom door, and then start running down the hall toward the exit. I dashed after him and scooped him up. He was crying hysterically and calling out, "I want my Mommy." This once calm, seemingly self-assured little boy was now an emotional wreck. Fortunately, by this time the other children were fairly well settled in, and I could devote a lot of my attention to Raymond and his adjustment to school.

HELP!

Sometimes children can fool us. It may take some children a little longer to react to a situation than others. In an effort to please, Raymond had done his best to come to school without crying. He could handle that level of emotional control for only so long. We must be sure to reach out and bond with all the children, even those who appear to have adjusted beautifully to the new environment. Their apparent adjustment may just be false bravado.

> Many children recognize when they are in a new environment and wisely respond with some hesitancy. It is only when they relax and feel comfortable that their true personality will emerge. Be careful not to judge any child's behavior or personality prematurely.

ASK YOURSELF:

Do you give all the children some special attention, even if they seem to be adjusting without any problems?

Do you recognize that once children settle in they may behave differently than they did during the first few days of school?

54. Accept a child's honest feelings

"YOU DON'T HAVE A MOMMY"

Toward the end of the first week of school, most of the children in my three-year-old class had settled in nicely. However, I still had one crier I tried to comfort as I carried her around the room. Lisa, with the biggest brown eyes I have ever seen in a child, came over to us and asked, "Why is that girl crying?" I explained that she missed her Mommy, and I understood that because I missed my Mommy too. Lisa's face broke into a knowing smile as she moved her head from left to right saying, "You don't have a Mommy." I replied, "Of course I do, would you like to see a picture of her?" By this time the crier had calmed down and was also curious about my mother. We walked over to my purse, and I pulled a photo of my parents out of my wallet. Upon viewing the picture Lisa responded indignantly, "That's not a Mommy, that's a Grandma."

HELP!

When a child says "I miss my Mommy," instead of denying or discounting those feelings we should acknowledge their validity. Tell the child that her parents miss her too, and they will see one another at the end of the day. Accepting children's honest feelings and then sympathizing with them is a much more positive approach than denial.

ASK YOURSELF:

Do you accept a child's honest feelings instead of denying or ignoring them?

55. Develop plans to comfort unhappy children

SOMETHING TO CLING TO

Curly-haired Nicholas, a two-year-old, was crying his eyes out. Mom had gone off to work, and he could hardly be consoled. Most of the morning, he wandered around the room tightly holding in his fist a crumpled photo of his mother in a wedding gown. Everyone who came in to visit the classroom was shown this photo and had to pause to admire it. It gave Nicholas a way to express himself. He certainly did not need to explain a thing to me.

HELP!

Separation anxiety is not unusual in two-year-olds. For some children it is harder to deal with than others, even if they have been in programs before. Having something important from parents or home to hold on to can help comfort the child. I have seen some parents give their child a key, telling the child, "I can't go home without you because you have the key." Others have left items, such as a favorite pin, pen, or trinket, for the child to take care of while the parent is away. We need to be careful that it is not something irreplaceable, as children can lose things, even treasured things.

♦ Another way to help unhappy children adjust is to suggest they do something, such as dictating a note to Mommy and Daddy telling them how they feel, or creating a piece of art for them.

ASK YOURSELF:

Do you have a plan to comfort and help unhappy children?

Do you make suggestions to parents about things they can do to help their child deal with the strain of separation?

56. Set up the easel to create a safe observation post

A SAFE ZONE

Kofi joined our class early in November. He spent a solid week planted firmly at the easel. While his mother was delighted that he was bringing home so much art work, I was a little concerned that he was not joining in any other activities. He would stand there, brush in hand, paying no attention to where the brush was going. Instead, he was busily observing everything going on in the room. How clever! He was in a safe zone. As long as he stayed at the easel, he did not have to interact with the other children. No one would ask him to share anything. No one would knock his structure down or try to take his toys away. This was a wonderful, secure observation post. Eventually Kofi felt comfortable enough to venture into other areas of the room and interact with the other children. He rarely painted again after that first week.

HELP!

Since that experience I always make sure to have my easel set up during the first two weeks of school. It provides the perfect safe zone for the child who needs a little extra time to observe before joining in activities. The child looks busy, and may chat with a passing child or adult, but is not forced to join in the thick of the action before he is ready.

If you are concerned about supervision and mess, you can always use washable Magic Markers or crayons instead of paints.

ASK YOURSELF:

Do you arrange the classroom with safe zones where children can observe the other children without having to interact with them before they are ready to?

57. Help children understand the daily schedule

IS IT TIME YET?

Without a doubt the most frequently asked question the first week of school is, "Is it time to go home yet?" We know young children cannot tell time. Answers, such as "in a little while," "at four o'clock," "later," "or not yet," are meaningless to children and eventually frustrate them. We can help by giving them a frame of reference they can understand.

HELP!

While young children cannot understand time, many are starting to understand sequence. Early in the day, and frequently throughout the day, explain the pattern of activities they can expect. Typically I will say, "We will play with toys, then have a story, then go on the playground, have lunch, nap, and sing some songs. After we sing songs it will be time to go home." This approach satisfies the children much better than the vague, incomprehensible response of "in a little while."

> Create a chart with pictures lined up in sequence that illustrate the schedule so the children can refer to it.

ASK YOURSELF:

Do you help children understand the daily schedule in ways that are simple enough for them to comprehend?

58. Use your name and the children's names often

NAMETAGS

I can't draw. One of the tasks I would dread at the start of the year was making nametags. I eventually found a pattern that resembled the body of a person and was simple to cut out. As an icebreaking activity on the first day of school, I would invite the children to decorate the nametags that I had pre-cut. This worked quite well with three- and four-year-olds.

Many teachers invest a lot of time and effort in making nametags, and when you think about it for a moment, they are of value only to the staff since most preschool children cannot read their own name, much less those of their classmates.

HELP!

 Since the children cannot read nametags, they can learn the names of the teachers and their classmates only by hearing them said often. For the first few days I will use phrases like, "Let Gwen help you with your coat," or "Let Gwen give you some juice." (There is a danger in this speech pattern. My husband gives me some pretty strange looks when I come home after a tough day and say, "Here, let Gwen get the potatoes for you.")

ASK YOURSELF:

Do you say your name and the children's names often to help everyone learn each others' names?

Do you use a child's name frequently all year long as a way to reinforce a strong self-image?

59. Wear pins or other accessories that appeal to children

NOVELTY PINS

One summer, my 10-year-old son attended a day camp. The highlight of the summer was the grand finale when the children presented their parents with gifts they had made. My son presented me with a pin, which I believe represented a teddy bear. It was a gift only a mother would love or dare to wear. I wore the pin for a solid week.

On the first day of school as I was preparing breakfast my son said, "Mom, aren't you going to wear the pin today?" It was the sort of request a mother cannot deny. I went upstairs and put the pin on.

As the children arrived at school they noticed the pin, which they easily recognized as a teddy bear. The children didn't know anything about me, but they knew about a teddy bear pin—it said a lot to them.

HELP!

Wearing little pins and accessories that appeal to young children can help you bond with children. They can also come in handy as a prop to facilitate conversations. In the following years, I collected a virtual zoo of inexpensive little pins, everything from dogs and dinosaurs to Grover and Winnie the Pooh. They have literally been worth their weight in gold to me.

> I still believe the most important thing you can wear is a smile.

The shortest distance between two people is a smile.

—Victor Borge

ASK YOURSELF:

Do you wear little pins or other accessories that will appeal to young children and help them bond with you?

60. Dress appropriately for working with young children

WHY SO SAD?

The people of Bolivia enjoy bright colors. The ladies living in the countryside wear traditional dress that consists of several layers of varying length skirts, topped off with a white blouse and a shawl that could only be described as a vivid rainbow caught on a loom. Most ladies wore a minimum of three different colored skirts. I saw layers of bright pink, yellow, turquoise, and light blue. At first, I thought I was seeing women on their way to a wedding or some special event. However, I soon learned that they wear these lovely garments every day, in the market, walking along the road, and tending their crops in the field.

One day our Bolivian guide, Carmen, asked me, "Why do Americans dress so sad?" I said I didn't understand her question. She explained that whenever an American tourist goes to buy a sweater (a very popular souvenir item) she always wants black, gray, or dark brown. I confess I had thought of looking for a gray sweater myself. She continued, "Why don't Americans like pink and yellow?" It was a provocative question. Do we think someone dressed in bright colors is somehow less smart, or less sophisticated?

HELP!

 As a teacher of young children, I dress for work, not just by wearing clothing that allows me to sit comfortably on the floor, and sensible shoes (in case I need to make a sudden dash across the playground), but also by the colors I wear. We do not work at a bank or insurance company where dark blue and gray are the expected norm. Our customers are young children, and we should dress to please them. Bright cheerful colors are all part of the image we should try to present. Dress happy and the children will notice.

ASK YOURSELF:

Do you dress appropriately for working with young children?

Do you wear clothing that allows you to sit on the floor, run across the playground, or accept a hug from a child who has just finished finger painting?

61. Count heads
frequently during the day

WHERE IS EVERYBODY?

Elaine seemed to be adjusting to school without any problems. She particularly enjoyed sitting in the sandbox outdoors. One sunny day in October I noticed Elaine was not in the sandbox. When I located her she was busy trying to climb over the fence. Fortunately she was better at making mud pies than climbing. I was lucky. A missing child is a teacher's worst nightmare. As a result of this frightening incident, I started counting heads almost constantly.

HELP!

We usually know where the noisy children are, or the ones most likely to succeed in getting into trouble. It is the quiet ones, the ones who seem to fade from view, that we might lose track of. They can wander out into the hallway, go visit another class, or perhaps—frighteningly—go beyond the school property. In some instances, it may be a long time before anyone realizes that they are gone.

To guard against losing track of a child's whereabouts, teachers should develop the habit of counting heads not just in September, but all year long. Count during free play, naptime, anytime, anywhere—in and out of the classroom. You should always know how many children are in your class at all times.

On one or two occasions I looked frantically for a child only to discover that I had miscounted, and no one was actually missing. You know how hard it is to count children who are constantly on the move!

> Do not assume the gate to the playground is locked. Visitors, parents, and others who enter or leave the school through the playground may forget to lock the gate behind them.

ASK YOURSELF:

Do you count heads frequently during the day in the class-room and on the playground? Do you count heads all year long, not just in September, to be sure that no one is missing or unaccounted for?

Do you check the gate on the playground to be sure it is locked before allowing the children to play outdoors?

Try This

Prepare a questionnaire for parents to fill out before school starts. The following are some of the questions you might ask:

- ☆ Does your child have any special needs, such as diet or allergies?
- ☆ Are there any family customs I should know about?
- ☆ Is your child afraid of animals, loud noises, being in the dark, or anything else?
- ☆ What toys does your child like to play with?
- ☆ Are there any games your child particularly likes or does not like?
- ☆ Does your child have any favorite books?
- ☆ Do you have any concerns or questions about your child attending school?
- ☆ What do you hope your child will gain from the school experience?
- ☆ Is there anything else you think I should know about you or your family?

To help parents get to know the staff and feel more comfortable, post pictures of everyone who works with the children in your class. Under each photograph add a short biography. This could include information on family, hobbies, education, and how many years she has been working with young children. Parents will no longer feel like they are with a group of strangers.

Try to have something very simple to make on the first day of school that the child can take home. Keep projects simple the first few weeks because you will undoubtedly be busy comforting some children.

To help children learn names, try this at music time. Have the children sit on the floor in a circle. Ask them not to cross their legs. Roll a colorful beach ball to each child while singing this phrase, "I roll the ball to Jamie; he rolls it back to me." To keep this activity interesting and exciting, do not go in a predictable pattern of each child in turn. Instead alternate children, or start with the first child on your right, and then the first child on your left as you work your way around the circle. Use a partially inflated beach ball because it will be soft and easy for the children to handle.

5

The Good, The Bad, And The Ugly

Creating a Team Relationship With Parents

Parents—can't live with them—can't live without them. Just as children come in all sizes, shapes, and personalities, some of which we relate to better than others, parents also run the gamut. There are those we really enjoy getting to know, and sometime in the future might consider them as social friends. Then there are a few who, when we see them heading our way, make us wish there were someplace to hide. A sudden, urgent need to go to the office or restroom is not an uncommon dodge.

We need to remember that as teachers we will have the responsibility of helping to educate a child for only a limited period of time. It is the parents who will play the critical lifelong role in the development of their children. The wise parent and professional teacher understand that they must do their best to get along with one another. In order to be effective, they must work well together as a team. Long before the first conference is scheduled, you should be working hard to establish positive relations with the parents.

I hope the following pages will give you some ideas of how to better understand and improve your relationships with parents— the good, the bad, and the ugly.

62. Help parents work through the natural tendency to be jealous

THE GREEN-EYED MONSTER—JEALOUSY

Jocelyn and I were curled up on a pillow reading a book together. When I finished it, she said, "Read it again, Mommy." When she realized what she had said she looked at me with an unsure smile, and we both shared a little giggle. She then said, "I mean Gwen." That was one of the nicest compliments I ever had from a child. I believe that she was so relaxed and comfortable that for just a moment she forgot where she was, and thought she was at home with her mother. While I treasured this moment, I did not share it with others, especially Jocelyn's mother.

HELP!

Parents struggle on the horns of a dilemma. On one hand they want their child to relate well to the teacher, and even bond with her. On the other hand, there is all this guilt about not being there with the child during the day and wanting to be sure that they are THE most important adults in their child's life. This combination of guilt and anxiety can create an insecure and overly sensitive parent. You can be sure that the child will mention the teacher's name at home and accidentally might even call Mom by the teacher's name.

A teacher cannot prevent this problem, but she can try to make it easier for the parents to bear. Occasionally let parents know that their child mentioned something about home, a special activity or a thing that Mommy likes. Honest comments help the parents feel important, remembered, and, hopefully, not in competition with the teacher for the child's affection.

♦ We must be careful to not overdo these comments as we do not want to add to the possible guilt feelings of parents who are unable to be with their child during the day.

ASK YOURSELF:

Do you help the parents work through the natural tendency to be jealous of the close teacher-child relationship you have established?

Do you remind parents that there will be many teachers in their child's life but only one MOM and DAD?

63. Put your personal feelings aside

MAKE LOVE, NOT WAR

Without a doubt the parent that challenged my skills the most was Sue. She rarely came to pick up her son, Harold, in person. She usually sent someone from her office or hired a driver who often arrived 15 to 20 minutes late. On the rare occasion that she personally came to pick up her son, she would get to school about 30 minutes early, sit down uninvited at my desk, eat a snack, and use the phone to catch up on her work. I managed to keep my cool and worked hard to have a good relationship with this person.

One day, one of the mothers brought her newborn infant to school to show the four-year-old class. The children asked the usual questions about the baby's sleeping, crying, and eating. When the mother talked about breastfeeding the baby, Harold was overheard to say in a rather discouraged way, "My Mommy still makes me do that." Fortunately, none of the other children heard the comment. What sort of razing would a four-year-old get for still being nursed by his mother? Now it is true that in some cultures children are weaned later than in others, but I felt confident that this was not a cultural issue. My sense was that this child was unhappy with the situation, and I decided to broach the subject with the mother.

When I mentioned Harold's remark to Sue, she smiled and said that she was still breastfeeding Harold. She explained that she derived great satisfaction from this activity, and really liked the feeling of closeness it gave to her and the child. Tactfully, I mentioned that it was my sense that Harold was not as happy about this arrangement as she was. Sue nodded her head in agreement. I also voiced concern about the potential for teasing if children, especially in kindergarten, became aware of the fact that Harold was still being breastfed. I then suggested that reading a book with Harold curled up on her lap would provide an excellent bonding opportunity. Sue listened carefully and left. A few weeks later, on one of her visits, she told me that she had stopped breastfeeding Harold, and was now reading books to him as they snuggled in a rocking chair.

HELP!

I have often thought that had I not controlled myself and gone the extra mile to keep a good relationship with this mother, I never would have been able to help Harold. For the children's sake, it is our duty to get along with all the parents so that, if necessary, we can talk to them about any subject. More important, because of the rapport we have established, they will be receptive to what we have to say. Sometimes this is very hard to do, but if your objective is to help children, then you must be able to relate in a positive way to all of the parents.

Parents have as important an obligation to try to relate positively to teachers as teachers do to parents. Trying to get to school on time, being prompt at pickup time, calling if there are any problems, and being courteous and thoughtful all go a long way to strengthen the bonds between parent and teacher that are so essential to the child's welfare.

Never hesitate to hold out your hand; never hesitate to accept the outstretched hand of another.

—Pope John XXIII

ASK YOURSELF:

Do you put your personal feelings aside and try your best to reach out to all parents in a positive way?

64. Make it easy for parents to confide in you

AN EXPERT

With all my training and experience, my two sons certainly gave me a run for my money. I can vividly recall standing at the foot of the stairs and calling (or screaming, depending on my level of desperation) up to them, "Why can't I get you two to go to sleep? I teach teachers, people come to me for advice, but I can't get you guys to do anything!"

HELP!

Mell Lazarus, the cartoonist who draws the popular comic strip "Momma," said, "The secret of dealing successfully with a child is not to be its parent." It is much easier to control yourself when dealing with someone else's child. The history, emotional bonds, and concerns about the future are quite different when it is your own child. We should remember this when talking with parents. The level of detachment that teachers have from children, and children have from teachers, is an important ingredient in the mixture.

I found over the years that telling stories about my missteps and frustrations with my own children helped parents feel comfortable with me. I was not perfect. I could snap or fail like any other human being. I believe this made it easier for parents to confide in me.

> Parents are more at ease and more likely to share their stories of failure and frustration with someone who has "Been there, done that" than with an "Expert."

> Learn to be a good listener. When parents confide in you, be nonjudgmental. Focus on strategies to help them deal with their child in the future.

We rarely confide in those who are better than we are.

—Albert Camus

ASK YOURSELF:

Do you encourage parents to seek your advice and counsel by being nonjudgmental and easy to talk to?

65. Learn about the culture and customs of the children's families

MISERY AT SNACK TIME

Jenny, from Thailand, spoke English and seemed to be adjusting to school nicely. She said good-bye to her parents with no problem. She participated in activities and played cooperatively with the other children. However, every day at snack time this child fell apart. She sighed, sobbed, and cried uncontrollably. At first I thought she did not care for the food we were offering. I tried to reassure her, and told her she did not have to eat it. I soon realized that it did not matter what was being served, even ice cream brought buckets of tears. The only way to stop this child's deep grief at snack time was to move her to another area of the room where she could compose herself. I arranged to talk it over with her parents.

When I chatted with her mother I asked, "What does Jenny say about school?" The mother grinned broadly and told me that she was very happy and couldn't wait to get to school each day. This pleased the parents very much. I said I was a bit confused because Jenny started to cry at snack time. Again, the mother smiled broadly and said, "Oh, that is nothing." I asked if she did this at home too. "Oh no," the mother said. She then explained that it was the custom in Thailand to spoon feed children until they were 10 or 12 years old. Thai parents consider it a loving gesture, a way to show their children how much they care for them. Poor Jenny, not only was I not spoon feeding her, the manners of a group of hungry four-year-olds reaching for food was not exactly for the fainthearted.

HELP!

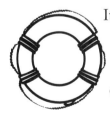
It is very important for teachers to learn about the children's home environment, their family's culture and customs so they can make the children as comfortable as possible. What we consider normal behavior may be frightening, insulting, or rude to someone from another culture.

ASK YOURSELF:

Do you make an effort to learn about the culture and customs of the families in your class so you can provide a supportive environment for the children?

Do you respect differences in customs and try to accommodate them?

66. Keep parents informed by posting lesson plans

WHAT'S GOING ON?

At almost every center, the menu listing the food for the week is prominently displayed. It is usually studied carefully. Children and parents congregate around the menu, find it very interesting, and discuss it together. It becomes a gathering place.

HELP!

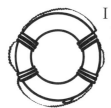

I believe that food for the mind is just as important to post as lunch menus. Parents want to know what activities are planned for the children. The daily schedule and the lesson plans for the week should be prominently displayed.

Posting lesson plans will help parents have more intelligent conversations with their children about what is happening at school. Of course, there must be a clear understanding on the part of the parents that schedules and plans are subject to change in order to be responsive to the needs of the children.

◆ In addition to the current week's lesson plans, I also post what's coming up in the next few weeks, and have been delighted with the parental support this has brought. Knowing the topics we will be talking about, parents have often sent in books and materials to share, helping me to provide a much richer classroom environment.

ASK YOURSELF:

Do you keep parents informed by posting lesson plans for your class?

67. Write meaningful newsletters

DIE OF EMBARRASSMENT

Redbeard is the title of a movie made by the famous Japanese director Akira Kurosawa. It tells the story of a kind and understanding doctor in feudal Japan. One incident involves a poor young boy who steals some food to feed his hungry family and is caught. Terribly distraught over the incident, the family drinks poison to save them from the shame and embarrassment their young son has caused. Of course, the good doctor is able to step in to avert a total tragedy.

Fortunately, most parents in American society deal with embarrassment in less drastic ways. However, we should not underestimate how hard it can be for some parents. Unreasonable expectations of their children's behavior and the ensuing embarrassment that results from this can be observed frequently.

I remember feeling as though a giant spotlight was on my table whenever I went with my children to a restaurant that was fancy enough to have tablecloths. Inevitably one of my sons would spill a glass of water; it was just a matter of time. Regardless of how understanding waiters or other patrons were, it took tremendous effort for me not to overreact.

HELP!

To help parents deal with potentially embarrassing situations, my November newsletter would advise: "Children are sometimes asked to dress in uncomfortable clothing, stay up later than usual, and control themselves well beyond their limited abilities, especially around holiday time. Please have reasonable expectations about your child's behavior."

Regular, timely newsletters are a very important part of parent education. They are a diplomatic, non-confrontational way to address issues of concern. A good newsletter is not just a listing of materials the school needs or a recitation of the previous month's art activities. Articles on child development and parenting should be offered as well.

I like to think that because of my newsletter, none of the parents considered committing hari-kari after attending a holiday party at the boss's house.

ASK YOURSELF:

Do you reach out to parents through a regularly published newsletter that includes articles and advice on child development and parenting?

Are your newsletters and other written communications distributed in a timely fashion?

68. Educate the parents as well as the children

EAVESDROPPING

During lunch hour I was doing a workshop on fostering creativity for the staff of a child care center. Out of the corner of my eye I noticed a mother standing by the door. At first I thought she wanted to talk to me, but then I realized that she was trying to hear what was being said to the teachers. Later this same mother stopped me in the hall and asked if I could do a workshop on fostering creativity for the parents.

HELP!

 Educating parents is an important part of a teacher's job. Workshops designed specifically for parents provide a golden opportunity for you to explain such topics as the value of block play and dramatic play, or the importance of stimulating creative thinking. Before scheduling a workshop, poll the parents to find out what times they are likely to be available and what topics they are interested in learning about. For those who cannot attend, provide a printed summary of the key points you make in the workshop.

If you have access to a video camera, consider making a videotape covering the material you present at the workshop. The parents could then borrow it and watch it at home. If the video includes scenes of classroom activity, it is bound to be a popular item.

ASK YOURSELF:

Do you conduct workshops for parents?

If parents cannot attend, do you provide a printed summary of the material presented?

69. Find ways to communicate with parents

NO NEWS IS NOT NECESSARILY GOOD NEWS

One program I was involved in used a bus service to deliver children to and from school. I felt isolated and uninformed each day as the children got off the bus. There was no daily contact with their parents, and so I had no information about the problems the children were facing. For example, who might be tired, hungry, or excited? At the end of the day, this feeling of isolation again took hold as I put the children on the buses that took them home. There was no opportunity to make a casual remark to a parent about an accomplishment, new friendship, or happy moment her child might have had that day.

HELP!

Drop-off and pick-up time is not when you should have a conference. However, a lot of information can be exchanged in the few minutes it takes to drop off or pick up a child at school. Mundane but important items affecting a child's behavior can be communicated, such as the child is feeling a bit under the weather, stayed up too late last night, or is excited about a visit from Grandpa.

Some parents have both car pool drop-off and pick-up arrangements. They almost never have to get out of their cars, and as a result they rarely see the inside of the building their child spends hours in, or their child's teacher. While it may be convenient, I think they forfeit a wonderful opportunity for invaluable casual contact and information exchanges between teacher and parent. Try to overcome the isolation that transportation arrangements can cause:

☆ Let parents know that they are always welcome to visit the class.

☆ If you do not have the opportunity to see parents on a frequent, regular basis, find alternate ways to communicate with them. Try e-mail, telephone calls, or short notes.

✩ To help you be more supportive and responsive to the children, encourage parents to contact you to alert you to any changes or special upcoming events that may impact their child or their family.

ASK YOURSELF:

Do you provide an atmosphere where parents feel free to visit their child's class?

Is communication with parents a two-way street, or is it limited to formal newsletters and notices?

Do you encourage parents to drop you a short note or send you an e-mail if they feel the need?

Are there times when you are available to talk with parents by telephone?

70. Do your best to calm an angry parent

STAY COOL

On a rather chilly morning in March, the children were arriving at school in the normal fashion. I suddenly heard a lot of shouting and screaming coming from just outside the three-year-old classroom. I raced right over to the area to find one of the mothers very agitated about what she called "Derek's negligent parents." In spite of the cold temperature, Derek had been brought to school by his babysitter wearing just shorts and a tee shirt with no jacket or sweater. This mother was yelling and trying to corner any passing adult to be the audience for her ranting. The shouting was disturbing the children and the poor parents who made the mistake of coming too close to the three-year-old classroom. I calmed the parent down, and we moved to a location away from the children where we could talk in private.

HELP!

At one time or another we all deal with angry people. In spite of what they are yelling about, you never really know what brought them to such a level of frustration. It could be anything—a flat tire, a headache, a business meeting that did not go well, or a mother-in-law extending an unwelcome visit. Whatever the cause, real or imagined, there is a technique called mirroring that can help to defuse the situation.

When you use mirroring, you just reflect back to the person what she is saying. This does not mean you are in agreement with her position, but it does mean you have heard her. For example, "You are very upset with Derek's parents; you feel they are not taking good care of him. You are worried about his health; you are concerned that he does not have a sweater on such a cold day." Notice, I did not agree with the mother's comments. All I did was repeat her words. Usually the parent will say, "Yes." Now you have an agreement of sorts; anger usually subsides with agreement. If the problem cannot be resolved immediately, then arrange a conference to deal with the subject in the not-too-distant future. Maybe by then the mother-in-law will have gone back home, and the parent will be in better spirits.

I have found this mirroring technique to be effective both in and out of school.

ASK YOURSELF:

Do you try to protect the children from adults who have lost their temper by inviting the adults to a place away from the children where you can talk privately?

Do you have a strategy for calming angry parents?

71. Involve parents in the school experience

FALSE BRAVADO

The second year I taught, I was at a cooperative nursery school. One of the requirements of a co-op is that parents work in the classroom on a regularly scheduled basis as assistant teachers. This keeps the tuition costs down, and by participating in the classroom the parents learn more about child development. The cooperative approach has both positive and negative ramifications. I certainly learned a lot in a hurry about dealing with parents.

Midyear we had an opening and accepted a little girl named Charlotte. Her mother was one of the most beautiful women I have ever seen. She had perfectly done hair at all times, even on windy, rainy days. She wore beautifully coordinated outfits and always looked like she had just stepped out of an advertisement in a glamour magazine.

The mother showed up for her co-op duties with a cup of coffee and a newspaper. She would help set up the snack and then retreat to a table, drink her coffee, and spend the next two hours with her head buried in the newspaper. I thought of her as arrogant—just too good for the rest of us. She made no attempt to join in activities or socialize with the children or the other adults.

HELP!

In the years since, I've often thought about what happened with this parent. In hindsight, I fear I failed her. What I took to be arrogance and a lack of interest could have been insecurity. This was a new situation for her, with new people and new responsibilities. It was obviously easier and less threatening to sit safely at a table drinking coffee and reading the newspaper than to be dealing with the children and adults. I am really sorry that I did not reach out to her more vigorously and try to ease the way for her to feel more comfortable and join in. Now whenever I see an over-confident adult, I keep in the back of my mind the idea that maybe it is all an act, so that we don't see the real insecurity underneath.

Don't always take someone at "face value." It could, after all, be a false face.

Reach out to help involve parents by asking them to go on class trips or visit the classroom for special activities. If their schedule does not allow time to join the class, then suggest other things they can do such as collect scraps of fabric, juice containers, and shoe boxes, or be part of a telephone chain. All the parents, even those with limited time and resources, should be invited to participate in their child's school experience.

ASK YOURSELF:

Do you make an extra effort to reach out to all the parents, even the ones that seem uninterested?

Do you offer suggestions to parents about how they can help the school?

72. Be willing to go the extra mile for parents

THE THINGS TEACHERS DO

Robert walked into class with his fingers wrapped tightly around some small object. After taking his jacket off, he came over to me, uncurled his fingers and held up a pair of shoelaces. He then said, "Mom said Gwen will put in the new ones." I was really steamed. The start of my day, checking lesson plans, setting up the room, and greeting children and parents wasn't busy enough, now I had to add threading shoe laces to my job description. Taking pity on Robert, I held my breath, and started cutting the 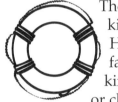 knotted old laces out of the black high-top sneakers that were well beyond ripe. Robert was absolutely delighted with his new shoe laces, and his mother never asked me to do anything out of the ordinary again. In fact, she volunteered for several class projects.

HELP!

 There are people who take advantage and even abuse the kindness of others. We find out who they are rather quickly. However, on occasion we should go the extra mile for a family. We never know all that is going on at home, and a kind gesture or favor can make all the difference to a parent or child.

ASK YOURSELF:

Do you put yourself out and occasionally do things that are not in your job description?

73. Show your appreciation to parents

TREASURE YOUR TREASURES

Wilbur was a very active, sociable young man. His father was always among the first to volunteer to help with class projects. He and his family were returning to their home in Australia in two days. While Wilbur was running on the playground, he tripped and fell. He had what appeared to be a small cut on his forehead, and there was a small amount of blood. I called the parents who came right over and picked him up.

The next day Wilbur came to school with four stitches over his right eye. What a souvenir from his year in the United States! His parents were both very understanding. "These things happen; he is an active boy," they told me reassuringly.

A year later, Wilbur's Dad was back in the United States to attend a conference and went out of his way to stop by to visit.

HELP!

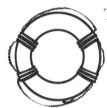

There are many gracious, understanding, and helpful parents. We should find ways to express our thanks to them. A personal note acknowledging their contribution of time and effort is a good way to start.

ASK YOURSELF:

Do you show your appreciation to the parents who go the extra mile for you?

74. Recognize that you may not be able to help every parent

EVERYONE COMES WITH BAGGAGE

Lee joined the four-year-old class in mid-October. She was a poised, self-confident young lady. The mother requested, and I agreed, that she could stay the first day to be sure Lee adjusted well. The child wasted no time at all in joining the other children in the various activities. Mom seemed a little awkward, but sat on a chair in the book corner. At the end of the day, I felt good about the smooth adjustment the child was making, and said that to the mother.

The next day when Lee was dropped off at school, she gave her mother a quick kiss good-bye and with a big smile on her face ran across the yard to join the children at play. Mom stayed at the gate for a few minutes, and then with her head bowed down, very slowly, almost reluctantly walked away. The same sort of parting scene occurred for the next two days. On Friday, Lee did not come to school.

The following Monday she was also absent. So, on Tuesday, I followed what was standard procedure for all children who were absent for a few days. I called the home to inquire about Lee's health and to say that we all missed her. The mother said that Lee had a cold but would be coming back soon. We did not see her again until the following Wednesday. Lee was again eager to attend school.

The next day the mother came with a gift for me. It was a flower in a small vase. She thanked me for being a good teacher, and then said she was withdrawing Lee from school. I was surprised, confused, and disappointed. I asked the mother if she would please sit down and talk with me for a few moments. Fortunately, there was adequate supervision on the playground, and I could afford that luxury.

I began our talk by observing that Lee seemed to be very happy at school. She appeared to enjoy the activities and being with the other children. The mother agreed, saying Lee liked school. I said I didn't understand what was happening. The mother started talking about her eight-year-old daughter, and how hard it had been for her to adjust to school. I listened carefully, and then tried to explain that Lee was a different person and appeared to be adjusting easily to school.

The mother leaned forward and in a very quiet voice said she knew what the real problem was. She explained that when she was a child, she had an extremely hard time separating from her mother, and now found it just too difficult to part with her own children. She realized that she was the one who had the problem.

I asked her how she had dealt with it with her older daughter. She explained that when the child became five years old she knew she would be in violation of the law if she did not send her to school, and this forced her to come to grips with her own emotions.

I congratulated her on overcoming her problem with the older daughter, and suggested that since she knew she could handle the separation, why not give Lee a chance right now? The child was obviously happy at school and would probably resent having to leave.

I am sorry to report Lee was withdrawn from our school. The mother assured me that when the time came (the legally enforced time) she would rise to the occasion and be able to leave Lee at school. I was disappointed that this mother did not allow her daughter to attend our school. I never saw Lee again.

HELP!

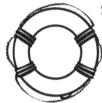

Sometimes the baggage that parents bring with them is well beyond the reach of a teacher to fix.

God grant me the serenity to accept the things I cannot change, the courage to change the things I can, and the wisdom to know the difference.

—Reinhold Niebuhr

ASK YOURSELF:

Do you accept the fact that, in spite of your best efforts, there will be some parents that you may not be able to help?

Try This

Educate parents by making them aware of:

- ☆ Articles and books to read on child development and parenting
- ☆ Upcoming lectures, discussions, and workshops in your community

Publicize live concerts, plays, and puppet shows designed for children.

Provide a list of books for parents to read to their children.

Prepare a booklet containing the words to songs you sing with the children during the course of the year.

Prepare a list of nutritious snacks for children to enjoy.

Put together a collection of recipes that are simple enough for children to help prepare at home.

Suggest family activities for the weekend:

- ☆ Go for a walk and collect leaves or rocks
- ☆ Go for a "listening walk"
- ☆ Go for a walk and look for things that are the color green
- ☆ Prepare simple food and then go on a picnic

Prepare a list of simple, developmentally appropriate games to play, such as Follow the Leader, or High Water Low Water.

Invite parents to come to class and share something special with the children:

- ☆ Play an instrument
- ☆ Read a story
- ☆ Help cook a favorite food
- ☆ Share a hobby

"Can We Talk?"

Making the Most of Parent-Teacher Conferences

Most educators agree with the statement that the most important people in children's lives are their parents. It would logically follow that frequent contact and communication between parents and teachers is the key to a good school experience for the young child. Unfortunately, most programs schedule only two conferences during the course of an entire year. The usual pattern is a 20- to 30-minute conference in the fall, and then again at the end of the year. I have seen programs that schedule 15-minute conferences. The parent hardly has time to warm the seat, much less relax and really communicate. This situation forces everyone involved to rely too heavily on the brief encounters at the beginning and end of the day when children are being dropped off or picked up. As a result, communication is often not as clear or diplomatic as it might be under other circumstances. I would like to see conferences scheduled more frequently during the year. I believe every three or four months would serve the parents, children, and teachers well.

A few days before scheduling conferences remind parents that the responsibility for a successful conference belongs to both parents and teachers. Suggest they think about what information they want to learn from you, what they want to tell you, and anything else they might want to talk about. A good conference is more than a friendly chat. Conferences are important, and both parents and teachers should prepare for them.

75. Control your conference schedule

OVERWHELMED

Most schools try to have all the parent conferences completed in one or two days. Many schools arrange for substitute teachers or even cancel classes for the conference day to try to make it easier on the staff. I was never satisfied with this arrangement. I found that, after three or four conferences with parents, everything started to blur. As hard as I tried to focus and concentrate, after a while I'm sure I sounded like a prerecorded message.

Some parents would arrive 10 minutes late and then stay for a full conference period. This would cause all the other scheduled conferences to be delayed, something that got progressively worse as the day dragged on. Finally, when the day was over I had trouble remembering all that had been said. This type of schedule just did not work well for me.

HELP!

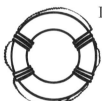

In order to give parents the benefit of a clear, fresh mind, whenever possible try to schedule no more than three conferences in a row. If there is no way around the full day schedule, be sure to build in 15-minute breaks so you can get up and clear your head.

Occasionally, this break time will be used up by a latecomer, but at least you avoid having angry parents lined up outside your door waiting for their turn.

> I strongly urge you to write down something about each conference. For every child, try to note what was discussed. You may be talking to 10 or more parents; they are talking to only one teacher. While you may forget what was said, you can be sure they will remember.

ASK YOURSELF:

Do you try to avoid scheduling too many conferences in one day?

Do you schedule breaks between conferences?

Do you write down notes on what was said during each conference?

76. Involve everyone
who comes to a conference

TWO'S COMPANY, BUT FOUR IS NOT A CROWD

Aditi's Dad had signed up for a one o'clock conference. I was waiting in the office when I heard a knock on the door. I was a bit surprised when I opened it and saw Aditi's Dad accompanied by two men and an elderly lady. I invited them in and was then introduced to Aditi's uncles and his grandmother. Not prepared for such a large group, I had to scurry about frantically looking for enough chairs to accommodate everyone. Since the father had invited all the relatives, and wanted them present, I had no objections. While the father did most of the talking, the other relatives did chime in on occasion. They were a lovely group to talk with. The interest shown by the family was very nice.

HELP!

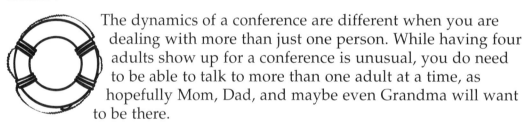 The dynamics of a conference are different when you are dealing with more than just one person. While having four adults show up for a conference is unusual, you do need to be able to talk to more than one adult at a time, as hopefully Mom, Dad, and maybe even Grandma will want to be there.

♦ Be sensitive to cultural differences.

♦ Be sure to direct questions and answers to all of the adults present.

♦ Don't allow one person to dominate and do all the talking.

You can get very interesting insights by listening to the different ways people respond to things. Quite often, you can help parents realize that they are sending a child mixed signals if Mom interprets or reacts to what the child is doing differently than Dad.

> I do not believe children should be present at conferences. They are a distraction, and these are conversations that they should not be a part of. Try to provide supervision for children in a nearby room.

ASK YOURSELF:

Do you ask questions and involve both parents in the conference, not allowing one or the other to dominate?

Do you provide supervision in another room for children during conferences, so parents can give you their undivided attention?

When you have a conference in your classroom, do you provide adult size chairs so your guests can sit comfortably?

77. Collect your thoughts
before responding to questions

PROPS

Many years ago, I watched an interview of Anwar Sadat, who was then President of Egypt. He was very relaxed, sitting in an overstuffed armchair. During the course of the interview he took the time to shake out his pipe, fill it with tobacco, and slowly light up. After taking several puffs, he continued with the interview. It was only later that I realized what had happened. Sadat was just so smooth that I doubt that it registered on many people. He had the pipe ready to go for just the right moment. When the correspondent asked a question that he was not prepared for, the one he needed a little time to think about and organize his thoughts—that's when the pipe business began. How clever; it did not appear that he was flustered or caught off guard, just that he was momentarily distracted by a need to light the pipe. Every time he paused to take a few puffs on this prop, I realized he was, in effect, buying some time to frame his response to a difficult question.

HELP!

I am not suggesting you start smoking a pipe, or anything else for that matter. However, having a prop such as a cup of coffee, glass of lemonade, or some munchies to snack on can prove very valuable. At the very least, it sets a friendly tone and makes for a much more congenial atmosphere. Guard against feeling pressured to give a quick response to a difficult question. When you are faced with something you want an extra second to think about, you can use a prop to buy time to collect your thoughts.

Needless to say, the drinks or snacks should be offered to all. I suggest carrot sticks, pretzels, grapes, or cereal mix for munchies. If you use donuts or chocolate, you will get depressed about the five pounds you are sure to gain.

ASK YOURSELF:

Do you try to create a cordial welcoming atmosphere for parent conferences?

When asked a question you are not prepared to answer, do you pause and collect your thoughts before responding?

78. Have a plan for each child

WHAT HAPPENS NEXT?

I can still recall my first conference as a parent. My son was in a three-year-old half-day program. The teacher was just delighted with him. She told me he was bright, cooperative, well coordinated, and just a pleasure to have in the class. Of course, I thoroughly enjoyed all the high praise she had for my son.

Driving home I was in good spirits, but I felt as though something had been missing. It was wonderful to hear about how great my son was, but I wondered what should happen next.

HELP!

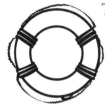
Telling parents that their child is doing beautifully, and we all adore him is not enough. There should be a plan of action or future goals for every child. For example, "Your child has shown an interest in mathematics, and we plan to develop this even further by . . ."

All parents are entitled to hear about your plans for their child.

Your plans for the class and individual children should be based on the knowledge you gain from careful observation and assessment. Only by doing observations and assessments regularly will you be able to create the proper learning environment for each child.

ASK YOURSELF:

Do you communicate a plan for the future development of each child?

Are observation and assessment of the children an integral part of your daily routine?

79. Ask open-ended questions to get parents to talk about issues

YOU SAID IT, NOT ME

Matthew couldn't get along with anyone. He knew how to throw a mean punch and had what one might politely call a short fuse. I was not looking forward to the scheduled parent conference. I wondered how I could discuss the subject without getting the parent to take a defensive position. Instead of saying something that might sound like an accusation, I decided to pose some questions to the mother. I asked, "Who does Matthew play with at home? Who does he play with when you visit friends or family?" She looked down and said he really didn't play too well with his cousins; they seemed to argue a lot. I complimented her on her observation skills and said, "You know, I've noticed the same thing here at school."

HELP!

By carefully and tactfully posing the right questions, I was able to get the mother to state the problem. Because I took this approach, I was not perceived as attacking her child, and the mother did not become defensive. As a matter of fact, I was in the enviable position of agreeing with the mother's statement. We could now work together to create strategies to be used at home and in school to help Matthew control his temper.

You are one step ahead of me if you are saying to yourself, "Yes, but what if the parent doesn't bring up the problem?" That is why I wrote the next story, Plan B, on that very subject.

ASK YOURSELF:

Do you use open-ended questions to get parents to talk about issues rather than just telling them about the problems you have in school?

80. Facilitate communication by relating specific observations

PLAN B

Having failed to get Elizabeth's mother, Ms. Tightlips, to talk about her daughter's behavior problems by posing several questions, I realized I had to move to Plan B. I always prefer the parent to be the first to broach a problem, but we all know that this does not always work.

I told her that yesterday during free play Elizabeth was busy playing quietly in the housekeeping area. Another child came into the area, picked up the toy dishes, and started to set the table. Elizabeth began yelling and pushed the other child out of the housekeeping area.

HELP!

 If you have a topic you wish to talk about or concerns about a child, be prepared to relate an incident you have observed and then use that as a basis for discussion. Be sure to describe what happened, using nonjudgmental language. This will reduce the likelihood of antagonizing the parent or giving her a reason to become defensive. It is much easier for parents to discuss a specific situation than their child's behavior in general terms. Most parents know if things are not going well with their children, and will gladly accept advice from someone they believe wants to help, but not from someone they feel is judging them.

ASK YOURSELF:

Do you relate specific observations to parents in order to facilitate communication?

Do you help parents avoid becoming defensive by appearing neutral and nonjudgmental?

81. Provide examples of a child's work

WORTH A THOUSAND WORDS

During a parent conference, teachers often struggle to try to describe the level at which a child is functioning. They resort to using vague phrases such as, "Your child does a wonderful job," "Your child needs to develop a little more," or "Your child is above average" (whatever that means).

HELP!

 When talking about small motor control and attention span you can illustrate your point by showing examples of the child's work. Try to save a few projects, for example, ones that involve cutting, pasting, or tracing, during the course of the year so the parents can see the progress their child has made. If you think a comparison would help, show examples of anonymous work from previous years. This avoids possible diplomatic problems with parents' comparing the work of child A to child B.

> If you have the luxury of a camera in the room, use it to take photos of block structures, cooperative dramatic play, or anything else that might help explain things to a parent during a conference. The old cliché that a picture is worth a thousand words sums it up nicely.

ASK YOURSELF:

Do you collect examples of the children's work to share with parents during conferences?

82. Ask parents what their child does when not in school

A BIT OF A BUSYBODY

Jamal was a very cheerful, happy-go-lucky four-year-old who was enrolled in my afternoon class. Every now and then he would have a hard day, when he seemed to be tired, cranky, and in a negative mood. When this happened with some regularity I started to keep notes. I quickly realized that this behavior usually occurred on Wednesday. After thinking about what might be different at school on Wednesdays, I decided I had to look elsewhere for a reason for the change in his behavior.

I arranged a conference with his mother and asked what Jamal did before coming to school. I was told he had a babysitter who watched him in the mornings, and he liked her very much. I then asked if the same pattern was followed every day. The mother said no, on Wednesday mornings he played next door. When I mentioned Jamal's shift in behavior she quickly realized what the problem was. Jamal was too tired for school after a full morning of vigorous play at the neighbor's house.

HELP!

It took several years of doing parent conferences before I was confident, bold, or frustrated enough (you pick the adjective) to start asking questions about the family and what the child did when not in school. We can't really understand the child's behavior if all we look at are the hours that he spends in a group situation at a center or school.

There is a very fine line between showing interest and being a busybody. Teachers must be careful not to invade anyone's privacy. I do believe a few inoffensive, carefully worded questions can give us a greater understanding of the child. After explaining this to parents, you can ask such things as:

- ✫ What does the child do before bedtime?
- ✫ What time does the child usually go to sleep?
- ✫ How is the dinner hour handled?
- ✫ Who does the child play with?
- ✫ What does the child like to play?
- ✫ How much television does the child watch?
- ✫ Do you use babysitters? When, and how often?
- ✫ How much contact is there with grandparents or other relatives?

Obviously, the questions that you ask should be tailored to what you need to know about a specific child in order to have a more complete understanding of how to handle any problems that may arise.

> Anything talked about during a conference should be considered strictly CONFIDENTIAL. Gaining and keeping a parent's trust is basic to the parent-teacher relationship.

ASK YOURSELF:

Do you invite the parents to share information about their child's playmates, activities, and home life?

Do you keep all information shared by parents strictly confidential?

83. Know what you want to say before contacting a parent to schedule an extra conference

TRAPPED

Yael, usually agreeable and calm, had been acting up quite a bit lately. Tears, as well as a few carefully delivered punches, were becoming all too commonplace. I wanted to chat with her parents to find out if anything was occurring outside of school that might help me understand this change in her behavior. Unfortunately, it was March and regular parent conferences were not scheduled for another couple of months.

When her mother dropped Yael off at school I asked if we could schedule a conference. She became very concerned and started peppering me with questions: "What was wrong, was Yael being a bad girl, was she having trouble doing work, was she getting along with the other children?" The mother was so stressed out that I could not delay the conference and found myself trapped. I had not yet prepared my thoughts carefully, but I found myself forced to stand there in the classroom, while other children and parents were arriving, and try to have a meaningful conversation with a now very upset parent. Obviously I could have handled this better.

HELP!

Occasionally, teachers need to schedule extra conferences for those times when they feel a need to share information, whether positive or negative. (There is a novel thought—a conference to share good news. Anyway, back to the subject at hand.) When you invite a parent to a conference, you can try to remove some anxiety by saying such things as, "Yael seems to be a little tired lately, nothing serious, just a change since the fall."

Most parents are very concerned about their children, and the request for an extra conference can send them into stress mode. Imaginations can run wild. As a parent, when I was invited to a conference I used to start speculating about what my son had done wrong this time. There is some comfort in narrowing the possibilities down. It might also help the parents to be better prepared and do some thinking of their own on the topic, so that the conference is more fruitful for both the parents and the teacher. How many times have we had meetings and an hour or two later thought of something we should have said?

Be prepared to talk about the subject if the parent can't handle waiting a day or two. Telling them you want to see them 10 days in advance is considerate of their schedule, but not of their psyche. Save them and yourself needless aggravation by being ready to discuss the situation once you broach the subject. Remember, you control the calendar, and you don't have to say anything until you are ready.

> Whenever you speak with someone, be aware of your surroundings. Guard against the possibility of children or other adults overhearing you. Parents have a right to expect you to act professionally and do everything you can to respect and ensure their privacy.

ASK YOURSELF:

Do you prepare yourself before mentioning to a parent that you would like to have an extra conference?

Do you try to arrange your schedule so the conference can be held as soon as possible?

Do you make yourself available when parents have a need to talk with you?

Do you respect everyone's right to privacy and avoid talking about children and parents in public?

84. Take more than enough time before expressing concerns about a child's development

THROW THEM A LIFE PRESERVER

This was one of those very serious conferences you hope you never have to have. George was a very personable young man and had the nicest of parents. I really enjoyed knowing all of them. However, I had serious concerns about George's development.

The news did not come as a shock to the parents. I had spent several months planting seeds of doubt, relating observations, trying to prepare the family, but not antagonize them. You may believe a child has special needs right off the bat, but if you say something to the parents too soon, they will dismiss it as prejudice, or say, "You just don't like my child." Only after months of observing the child and bonding and establishing trust with the parents can you broach this sort of subject.

There were tears, as the parents listened to my concerns. I tried to be as understanding as possible without letting them stay in a comfortable state of denial. I then offered them a sheet of paper with the names and phone numbers of several professional people who could help.

HELP!

As a teacher, if you have the sad task of needing to express concern about a child's development, be sure you are not too hasty. This must be approached very carefully and deliberately. Do not underestimate what you are doing. This is traumatic and devastating news for any parent. What you have to say can turn a family upside down. Never say anything until you have talked with other professionals on the staff, discussed your concerns, invited them to observe, and had them confirm your observations. Take your time.

Your job is not over once you share your concerns. It is essential that you have suggestions and professional references for the parents. Giving news like this is akin to throwing them overboard in the middle of the ocean. You must offer them some life preservers—people and organizations they can contact for help.

One or two weeks after the conference, be sure to check with the parents to see what progress they have made, and if they need additional help.

Words once spoken can never be recalled.

—Wentworth Dillon

ASK YOURSELF:

Do you take more than enough time before sharing concerns with parents?

Do you ask other professionals on the staff for input?

Do you offer parents resources they can contact for help?

Do you follow through and after some time ask if they have made any progress?

85. When necessary, encourage parents to request testing or see a specialist

PEDIATRICIANS

About two weeks after I spoke with George's parents, the mother came in to see me. She was just beaming with a broad smile; she had faced the problem and now felt good about things. During her last visit to the pediatrician, she asked the doctor her opinion of George. I rather imagine the doctor patted the child (and maybe even Mom) on the head and said, "He's fine." Thereby undoing all the work I had so carefully laid out.

HELP!

 I think pediatricians are terrific. They work long, hard hours and deal with myriad problems. However, consider the circumstances of a typical visit. The child is running a fever, is perched high atop an examination table, probably half undressed, with Mom, a nurse, possibly a needle, and the doctor hovering nearby. This hardly simulates a normal social scene. Pediatricians know a lot, but they rarely have the opportunity to observe a child's attention span, self-control, or social interactions in a normal setting.

If you are counseling parents about a problem, suggest they get their child tested or go to a specialist. Explain that their pediatrician may not be the best person to consult because of her lack of specialized training and the limited opportunities she has had to observe their child. On the other hand, if the parents have accepted the idea that help is necessary, asking their pediatrician for references is a good idea.

ASK YOURSELF:

Do you encourage parents to see a specialist or request testing if there is a concern?

86. Avoid using labels

DON'T TAKE THE BAIT

I had some concerns about Zachary. His speech was not appropriate for his age, and he seemed very inattentive. My guess was that there was a hearing problem that was affecting his speech pattern. Poor hearing can translate into an inability to reproduce sounds, and not hearing can be misinterpreted as a lack of comprehension or just being inattentive. In spite of my best guess as to what the problem was, I did not label it.

At the conference, the parents wanted to know what was wrong. They asked, "Did Zachary have ADD, was he mentally retarded, did he have a learning problem?" I did not know for sure, but more important, I was not trained or qualified to answer those types of questions. All I could do was recommend a good screening.

HELP!

 A teacher can usually tell when a child does not fit in the normal range, but opinions as to what the specific problem is go beyond the scope of most teachers' training and expertise.

> Be careful that when a parent presses for answers, you do not take the bait and label the child.

It is our obligation to tell parents we are concerned that their child is not functioning in the normal range, but it is wrong to go beyond that. Recommendations for screening and evaluations will put parents on the right track to getting help for their child.

> Try to arrange hearing and vision screenings for all the children.

Don't let what you cannot do interfere with what you can do.

—John Wooden

ASK YOURSELF:

Do you carefully avoid using labels?

Do you remind parents that you cannot diagnose children as you are not trained or qualified to do so?

87. Prepare yourself
for negative reactions

DENIAL—TAKING THE FIRST STEP

When people get bad news, the natural reaction is to go into denial. For example, if they have to face the horror of being told by a doctor that they have cancer, the typical first reaction is, "There has been a mistake. Let's recheck this." After additional tests, and time, the patient starts to accept the diagnosis, and only then is ready to deal with the possible treatments that may be available.

I doubt that anyone upon hearing such horrible news would throw their arms around the doctor, give him a hug, and say, "Thank you for telling me. Now I can get right on top of things and take care of this as soon as possible." More than likely the patient would be upset and angry with the doctor, thinking there was an error, or wondering why the doctor hadn't discovered the problem sooner.

HELP!

When told something troubling, parents will become upset. Teachers need to prepare themselves for the very unwelcome responses that they are likely to have to endure.

A common reaction is for the parent to withdraw the child from school, using logic that says, "They never liked my child in the first place, they don't like me, they think everyone has a problem. The teacher is incompetent and lazy, and just doesn't know what to do."

Many teachers decide it is easier to just ride things out. They rationalize their decision by saying the school year will end; there will be a new class and new teacher in a few months, so why rock the boat and risk negative reactions? It is a difficult decision, but if your concern is the well-being of the child, then you cannot look the other way.

It is true the parents may deny the problem, may withdraw their child from the school, and may say nasty things about the staff. You can take comfort in the fact that you are laying the groundwork for the future. When the next caring professional accepts the obligation to alert the parents to a potential problem, can the parents explain it away again? How many times can they look the other way? It is not very satisfying, but you will have made it easier for someone down the road to be believed and to start getting the proper help for the child.

> Do not wait for the parents to come say thank you—that is expecting too much. Your satisfaction must come from within.

The time is always right to do what is right.

—Martin Luther King, Jr.

ASK YOURSELF:

 Do you recommend that parents get help for their child, even if you think your recommendation will draw a negative reaction?

88. Have a game plan for conferences

HOW TO END IT ALL

The first few years of my career, I had problems ending my parent conferences. They seemed to go on forever. We would have a good discussion about a child and then the conversation seemed to move on to other subjects. I can recall talking about everything from the weather to diets and even the political situation of the day. (That's from my years in Washington, D.C.) This caused me to get off schedule, and I always seemed to be running late for my next conference.

After a while, I concluded that the parents did not want to be rude and cut me off, in case I had more to say, so they just kept talking about anything under the sun. I came to realize that it was the teacher's job to signal that the conference was over.

HELP!

A parent conference should have a game plan. I like to think of it as having a beginning, middle, and end. You as the teacher set the tone. Try to begin with a positive comment about the child and then ask a general (non-threatening) question such as, "Who does Philip like to play with?" or "Which children does Philip talk about at home?" The answer to this can be fascinating. They do not always mention the names you would expect. This question indicates to the parents, right off the bat, that you want to know information from them, and you are encouraging them to talk.

A conference is a failure if only one party does the talking. It should be a sharing or exchange of information.

Some parents will want to talk about their other children. While this is very flattering, I usually decline. Not to be rude, I tell them that I am uncomfortable talking about a child I have never observed and about circumstances I am unfamiliar with. Just as you would not want someone in elementary school second-guessing you, you should not be second-guessing someone else. Call it professional courtesy, or in plain English, minding your own business.

The middle and final sections of the conference deal with what the parents are interested in, the teacher's observations and the plans the teacher has for their child's future. Try to end the conference on a positive note. You want the parents to feel that together you have worked out a plan for the next several months.

So how do you end it? I have found body language does the trick nicely. Remember the parents do not want to be rude and cut you off, so you must signal clearly that you have said all that you wanted to. I do not do this until after I have asked the parents one last time if they have anything else they wish to talk about. When I am certain we are both through communicating, I do one of the following:

- ✰ Wiggle in my chair
- ✰ Swivel as though I am about to get up
- ✰ Close a book
- ✰ Turn over a paper
- ✰ Pack up my materials
- ✰ Stick out my hand to shake hands
- ✰ Stand up

I really want to share one other experience on this subject. One year, I had a troubled boy named Wayne in my class. I had tried my absolute best for 30 minutes to get the mother to open up and discuss the child, but I had failed. The conference was now over, we were standing, and the mother had her hand on the door. I guess you would have to say it was the last possible moment. The mother turned to me and started to cry, she opened up her heart, and at last was ready to talk. It was one of the best conferences I ever had. We stood there sharing our thoughts for well over half an hour (I was afraid to move and change the dynamics.)

> It is never over; we must always be ready to listen.

ASK YOURSELF:

Do you have a game plan for conferences?

Do you help parents stay focused on the child?

Do you end on a positive note?

Do you end the conference only when both parties have communicated all that they wish to?

Try This

Be sure to have chairs available for parents who are waiting for their conference. While they wait, you can provide the following:

- ☆ TV with a video on child development or parenting
- ☆ TV with a video of the class in action
- ☆ A photo album of the children participating in class activities
- ☆ Early childhood education journals and parenting magazines

Start a resource file. Collect articles from journals and magazines on topics that would be of interest to your parents. For example, articles on developing literacy, the importance of play, sibling rivalry, bedtime routines, and good nutrition. Share these with parents as appropriate after the conference. It is less confrontational and easier to make your point when an expert discusses the issue. Parents will appreciate having something to take home to read.

Arrange a follow-up call with the parents for after the conference. This allows you to check on progress and reevaluate any suggestions or strategies you discussed.

Afterword

If you have classroom stories, ideas, or suggestions that you would like to share, I would love to hear from you. Please e-mail them to me at gwenkaltman@hotmail.com. Be sure to include your name, so that you can be acknowledged if your material is included in a future publication. Thank you for sharing!

Resources

Help Yourself: Creating Your Own Plan for Improvement

The best way I know to ensure continued growth throughout your career is to try new things and develop the ability to honestly evaluate your own work. In those areas that you determine you can do better, reread the chapter and then use the form on the next page to plan your strategy for improvement. I urge you to take your time. Please do not rush quickly through the book. You are trying to develop new skills and in some instances a change in attitude that will become a part of who you are. This takes time and consistent effort.

As you develop the skill to analyze your own work—no simple feat—you will be creating a powerful tool for self-improvement. When you do your self-evaluation, remember to consider not only what went wrong but also what went right. Be sure you note the date on your form and keep it as a reference for future years. I suggest that you repeat this process every year, as you are sure to change and evolve.

If your initial attempts do not work as well as you had hoped, do not be discouraged. What is important is that you are learning about yourself and developing your skills as a teacher. Children are pretty resilient. If an activity or approach does not work out quite the way you envisioned it, the children will survive the experience and so will you!

No one knows what he is able to do until he tries.

—Publilius Syrus

Improvement Plan

Date: Chapter:

Ask yourself:

My plan for improvement:

_____

My initial observation (evaluate the children's response):

My second observation (if applicable):

Reflections:

Based on your observation(s), what part of your plan worked well?

How would you modify it in the future?

What other ideas or strategies could you try?

Helpful Organizations

Association for Childhood Education International
17904 Georgia Avenue, Suite 215
Olney, MD 20832
(301) 570-2111
http://www.acei.org

Child Care Information Exchange
PO Box 3249
Redmond, WA 98073
(800) 221-2864
http://www.ccie.com

Child Development Associate
Council for Professional Recognition
2460 16th Street, NW
Washington, DC 20009
(800) 424-4310
http://www.cdacouncil.org

Clearinghouse on Early Education and Parenting
University of Illinois at Urbana–Champaign
Children's Research Center
51 Gerty Drive
Champaign, IL 61820
(217) 333-1386
http://ceep.crc.uiuc.edu

Head Start Information and Publication Center
Head Start Bureau
Administration for Children and Families
U.S. Department of Health and Human Services
1133 15th Street, NW, Suite 450
Washington, DC 20005
(866) 763-6481
http://www.headstartinfo.org

National Association for the Education of Young Children
1509 16th Street, NW
Washington, DC 20036
(800) 424-2460
http://www.naeyc.org

National Association for Family Child Care
5202 Pinemont Drive
Salt Lake City, UT 84123
(801) 269-9338
http://www.nafcc.org

National Association of Child Care Professionals
PO Box 90723
Austin, TX 78709
(800) 537-1118
http://www.naccp.org

National Child Care Information Center
Child Care Bureau
Administration for Children and Families
U.S. Department of Health and Human Services
243 Church Street, NW, Second Floor
Vienna, VA 22180
(800) 616-2242
http://nccic.org

National Network for Child Care
Cooperative State Research, Education, and Extension Service
U.S. Department of Agriculture
1400 Independence Avenue, SW
Washington, DC 20250
(202) 720-7441
http://www.nncc.org

Southern Early Childhood Association
PO Box 59930
Little Rock, AR 72215
(800) 305-7322
http://www.southernearlychildhood.org

Zero to Three
National Center for Infants, Toddlers and Families
2000 M Street, NW, Suite 200
Washington, DC 20036
(202) 638-1144
http://www.zerotothree.org

Suggested Reading

Bailey, B. A. (2000). *Conscious discipline: Seven basic skills for brain smart classroom management.* Oviedo, FL: Loving Guidance.

Barbour, A., & Desjean-Perotta, B. (2002). *Prop box play: 50 themes to inspire dramatic play.* Beltsville, MD: Gryphon House.

Coughlin, P. A., Hansen, K. A., Heller, D., Kaufmann, R. K., Stolberg, J. R., & Walsh, K. B. (1997). *Creating child-centered classrooms: 3–5 year olds.* Washington, DC: Children's Resources International.

Dodge, D. T., Colker, L. J., & Heroman, C. (2002). *The creative curriculum for preschool* (4th ed.). Washington, DC: Teaching Strategies.

Dodge, D. T., & Phinney, J. (2002). *A parent's guide to preschool.* Washington, DC: Teaching Strategies.

Eliason, C. F., & Jenkins, L. T. (2003). *A practical guide to early childhood curriculum* (7th ed.). Upper Saddle River, NJ: Prentice Hall.

Hendrick, J. (2001). *The whole child: Developmental education for the early years* (7th ed.). Upper Saddle River, NJ: Prentice Hall.

Jervis, K. (Ed.). (1989). *Separation: Strategies for helping two- to four-year-olds.* Washington, DC: National Association for the Education of Young Children.

Weitzman, E., & Greenberg, J. (2002). *Learning language and loving it: A guide to promoting children's social, language, and literacy development in early childhood settings* (2nd ed.). Toronto, ON: Hanen Centre.